California Wine

A Sunset Pictorial

California

LANE PUBLISHING CO. • MENLO PARK, CALIFORNIA

Wine

Edited by:
BOB THOMPSON

Photographer:
TED STRESHINSKY

Design, Maps, Drawings:
JOE SENEY

Coordinating Editor:
SHERRY GELLNER

  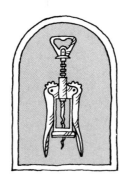  

Historic Photographs

The historic photographs are by the courtesy of: Philo Biane (46, 47, 55, 56, 57); Browne Vintners (85); Korbel (111); C. Mondavi & Sons (143 top left); Schramsberg Champagne Cellars (143 bottom); St. Helena Star (144 right); United Vintners (115 top); Wine Institute (54, 84, 95, 99, 100, 110 left, 114, 117 top, 122, 141, 142, 143 top right, 144 left, 177); and Young's Markets (109).

Front Cover: White wine glows against the wintery background of mustard in a California vineyard. Photograph by Fred Lyon.

Back Cover: Jesuit Brother checks casks in Novitiate of Los Gatos Winery. Photograph by Ted Streshinsky.

Executive Editor, Sunset Books: David E. Clark

Second Printing (Updated) March 1977

Contents

Introduction

Suddenly, in the past 10 to 15 years, people in other parts of the world have begun to find out what Californians have known for a long time: that this state makes very good wine.

This era of discovery coincides with the first lengthy period since the turn of the century in which California winemakers have been left in peace to do the kind of winemaking they would like to do.

Commercial winemaking began in California in the 1830s, but did not have much audience until the Gold Rush of 1849 exploded the population. By 1880 a vine louse called phylloxera had become almost as devastating a force in California as it had in Europe.

Before a cure for this natural plague could be found, Carrie Nation and her kind had managed to make Prohibition seem like a good idea. Making commercial wine was illegal from 1919 through 1933.

Although winemaking became legal again in the latter year, it hardly became attractive. The long years of Prohibition had done away with most of the fine vineyards in the state. The depths of the great Depression did not offer an optimistic environment for heavy investment in new vineyards or equipment.

As the country recovered from Depression it fell into World War II, which caused the government to requisition a considerable part of several grape crops (for raisins, even for industrial alcohol) and a good part of the manpower.

Having started 5800 years behind Europe, and having run on a rough track most of the way since, California's winemakers have been forced to rely on science to do much of their catching up.

The revolution since the 1950s has reached into every corner of the state's vineyards and wine cellars. Old

TIME OF CHANGE. California wine dates back to the Mission era. Throughout its history in California, winemaking has grown steadily, but slowly. Now, however, the pace has accelerated tremendously. Vineyard acreage has almost doubled within the decade. So has the capacity of the wineries.

vineyards are being replanted to new grape varieties. New vineyards are springing up where no grape ever grew before. New wineries are opening at a matching rate, equipped with casks, presses and other gear drawn from every corner of the globe, but only rarely with owners drawn from other countries.

With change a daily fact of life, this is no time to make lasting judgments on what California wine is. Likely it will be something different by tomorrow. But this is a fine moment to capture impressions of some of the old faces that have brought California wine this far, and some of the new faces that will take it to some new level.

California Wine is Sunset's effort to catch the flavor of this turbulent era of achievement. For the purpose, we chose to photograph the vintage of 1972 from first leaf to new wine in the bottle. As fate would have it, 1972 would prove once more that not every year is a vintage year in California. Much of the harvest came to the wineries cold and wet after a frosty spring and a searing summer. Ah, well. The Europeans have always said that wine loves a struggle. No wonder it loves California.

For their unstinting help, we thank all of the state's winemakers and their staffs. We particularly wish to thank Michael Biane, Norman Bundgard, Paul Draper, Russell Green, Alice Heitz, J. E. Heitz, Thomas Kruse, Jean Perry, Dr. Richard Peterson, Prof. Vincent Petrucci, Jose Rojas, August Sebastiani and Laurie Wood; and California State University-Fresno, Flynn Tree Service, the University of California-Davis, the Upright Harvester Company, Vintage Nursery, and The Wine Institute of California.

We regret only that limitations of space did not allow us to show every winery in California.

A Vintage Year

THE JOY OF SHARING. At Heitz Cellars, friends toast the harvest with a communal bowl of newborn wine.

THAT'S MY BABY. Joe Heitz evaluates his fledgling Grignolino Rosé.

The day winemakers wait for is that
autumn day when the last of the
new vintage is safe in the cellars.
Then they can pause, gather friends, and
toast the new wine. But a vintage
is not just the gift of a handful of autumn
days when the grapes are harvested.
A vintage begins in March
with the first swelling of leaf buds in
the vineyards.

BUD BREAK. The first soft leaf unfolds on a vine as soon as a warm spell comes in March.

March

Perilous infancy

In mid-March the bare bones of winter suddenly develop a patchy fringe of green as the buds swell, then burst open to reveal a pale wreath of leaves no more than an inch long. Each variety has its own timetable. The early bloomers will be the first grapes picked in the fall, and the late ones will go to the crushers last.

March through May is a perilous season for the fast-growing, tender shoots. One night of spring frost can diminish the harvest by 10 percent. Thirty straight nights of freezing can wipe out whole vineyards as the crop is cut in half for the year. Generally the coast valleys are most susceptible to frost, but 1972 proved that no part of the state is completely free of the threat.

EARLY GROWTH. The limber green wood of
new canes begins to appear behind the
leaf stems before March gives way to April.
From April through June, canes grow
very rapidly if all goes well with the weather.

THE MOVING FINGER BITES. Frost strikes
with complete whimsy—sometimes at one
point in a vineyard, sometimes at another. At
dawn after a night of frost, the vines look
normal. But with the first warming rays of
the sun, damaged leaves shrivel and darken.
   Growers fight frost with orchard heaters,
big blowers, or mist but can only cut
their losses, not eliminate them altogether.

June

Blossomtime

GRAPE FLOWER INFANT BERRIES

TIME TO GROW. Almaden vines at Paicines soak up the last warmth of a soft spring evening.

By mid-May the fruit buds look very much like clusters of miniature grapes. Then, in the middle third of June, these buds unfold into one of the truly insignificant floral displays in all of botany. Though not a feast for the eyes, this flowering marks a critical stage in growing wine grapes. To set a full crop, the vines must have 10 to 14 days of dry, moderately warm weather. Rain is a disaster. Extreme heat is not much better. Once the fruit sets, berries form quickly. A vineyardist is having a good year when he can afford to thin his fruit for quality.

AFTER THE RAINS. Weeds disappear from Mont LaSalle vineyards.

AIR POWER. Rolling compressors take some travail out of grooming a young Almaden vineyard.

Starting in spring

The ripening sun

Late spring and early summer tell newcomers whether they really want to be vineyardists or do not, for these are the months of no romance at all. Stubborn canes need tying. Sucker canes have to be removed from each plant. (Although pneumatic clippers are a great improvement over hand-powered models, nobody has yet figured out a way to save the stooping over.) On some varieties, in some places, the foliage has to be thinned to let more sun shine onto the forming fruit. Two or three applications of sulfur have to be sprayed on to guard against mildew.

Inevitably a no-breeze hot spell adds its weight to the chores, but vineyardists expect to trade sweat in June for ripe grapes in October.

FASTEST GUN IN THE WEST. Worker staples trellis wires.

RITES OF SPRING. Before the end of May, vines lose their energy-sapping sucker canes.

GETTING SET. Cellarman at Chalone Vineyard in Monterey readies presses for the harvest.

July 🍇

Clean-up, paint-up, fix-up

Most of the gear wineries use to harvest grapes and ferment new wines lies idle from October until the following September, gathering rust in winter and dust in summer. July is clean-up, paint-up time. Grape gondolas, crushers, and presses get scrubdowns and new paint. Fermenting tanks are washed as if they were dinner plates. Tanks that will hold new wine get washed down and sterilized with sulfur. Vines stop growing and fruit begins to mature by late July.

BIG WASH. Cellarman at Barengo winery in Lodi washes down a 30,000-gallon redwood tank.

GETTING READY. Purple tinge announces
that grapes are ripening.

THE QUIET WAIT. Most wines slumber through the summer, as does a Chardonnay at Hanzell in Sonoma.

August 🍇 *Hurry up and wait*

In theory wine grapes will be ripe for picking 50 days after the first blush of color in their vineyard. In practice the fruit ripens in 45 days (late August) or takes 80 (which means November). Throughout this period vineyardists, haunted by spectres of early rain and cold, try to convince winemakers to pick quickly. The winemakers counsel patience, hoping for the superlative. Otherwise, a little wine goes into bottles and a lot into winetasting tourists.

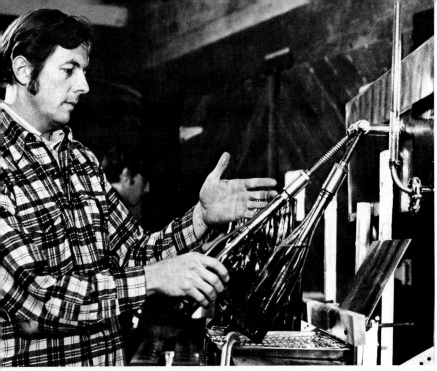

SPACE RACE. At Stony Hill in the Napa Valley, filling 300 bottles means one more oak cask is empty and ready for the new vintage.

FIRST-HAND LOOKS. Tours and tasting attract summer throngs to wineries, including Beringer.

BY DAWN'S EARLY LIGHT. Two pickers run to empty pans of Chenin blancs in a Charles Krug vineyard.

September  *Harvest!*

STILL GOING STRONG. A day ends around 4 p.m.

The vintage builds toward its peak as September moves toward its close.
A few varieties of grapes ripen early in the month, a few straggle into
late October, even November. But most California grapes ripen in the
last three weeks of September and the first three of October.
At the peak of the harvest, pickers go into the vineyards before the sun
gets up, racing in the cool dawn air so they can go slower in the heat of
the day. Some small vineyards still pick into the time-honored lug boxes.
Most crews empty lug-sized pans into big gondolas holding two, three,
even five tons. In recent years mechanical harvesters have replaced hand
picking on many of the sizeable ranches in California.

TO BE OR NOT TO BE. Wine's loss is honey's gain.

September

The competition

One reason a winemaker celebrates the harvest is physical victory. He faces earnest competition for his ripe grapes. Birds eat a fair part of the crop. Bees are less dramatic but hardly less damaging. As if winged marauders were not enough, deer will eat everything but the trunk of a vine every chance they get. Weather is another question altogether, to be worried over the year around.

A HARD BIRD TO LOVE. Starlings take every grape the pickers missed at Winery Lake Vineyard in Napa.

October 🍇

The tumult of birth

The crushing of grapes to make wine is a messy operation. Ton upon ton of pulped fruit cannot be altogether attractive. Still, as soon as the fermentations get going, matters begin not only to look better but to smell just fine. A fermentation that smells sweet and fresh is almost sure to yield wine worth drinking no matter if it does not come from the vintage of the century. Demands upon the winemaker are incredible. He must help each grape variety follow its distinct path in fermenting, even in the middle of the night; he must also schedule arrivals of new grapes to coincide with the availability of crushers, fermentors, and the rest of his equipment.

ON THE WAY TO WINE. Grapes move into the crushers at Brookside.

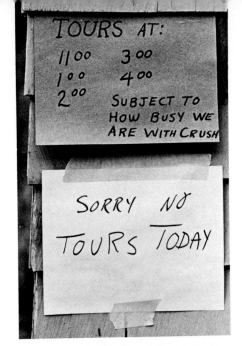

SIGN SAYS IT ALL. The vintage is busy.

FOR COLOR'S SAKE. Red wines are pumped over the cap of skins to gain color. The winery is Simi.

FINISHING TOUCHES. A rain-chilled picker (right) gathers the last of the Cabernet Sauvignon for the crusher at Mt. Eden (lower left). In the coast counties, the end of the harvest often is signalled by the first rain falling on the last Cabernet grapes. A Napa picker (lower right) has a somewhat warmer day of it.

THE REWARD. When new wine tastes good, the work was worth it.

October

High-point and mid-point

Finally, as October winds down, so does the tempo of the harvest. Between the emptied vineyard and the full cellar there is time to celebrate the vintage . . . to raise a festive bowl to having escaped the frost, the hot spell and the deer . . . to toast getting in ahead of the fall rains . . . but mainly to toast the new wine for itself. The lull cannot last, though. There are infant wines and aged vines to care for.

COLOR-CODED CARPET. Leaf colors advertise differing grape varieties in blocks of Napa Valley vines.

November 🍇 The ebbing flame

One hard rain after the harvest, color comes to the vines.
Chardonnay leaf turns the most delicate of yellows. Cabernet
Sauvignon turns a bright crimson. Petite Sirah goes dark,
almost purple. The autumn leaf colors of each variety bear an
inexact relationship to the color of the ripe grapes, and
a more distant relationship to the color of the wines. All are
pigmented by distinctive combinations of the same compounds
that color garden flowers. Old vineyards mount the showiest color.

SLEEPY VINES. Color betrays advancing dormancy in the vineyards.

READING LEAVES. These colors typify Chardonnay, Zinfandel, and Cabernet Sauvignon.

Starting in December

Season of marriages

After fermentation finishes early in December, new wines are pumped from one tank to another for the first of several times. The process, called racking, clarifies the wine by leaving grape solids behind. Lab technicians run dozens of tests to pinpoint the strengths and weaknesses in each wine. And the winemakers begin to taste—the ultimate assessment. Winter is also a time to make blends from new wines or old. In the romantic language of wine, a blend is a marriage. As marriage broker, the cellarmaster makes dozens of miniature samples. The combination he likes is reproduced in full volume in the cellars.

FOR CLARITY'S SAKE. Mirassou cellarmen rack a Cabernet Sauvignon that has fallen bright.

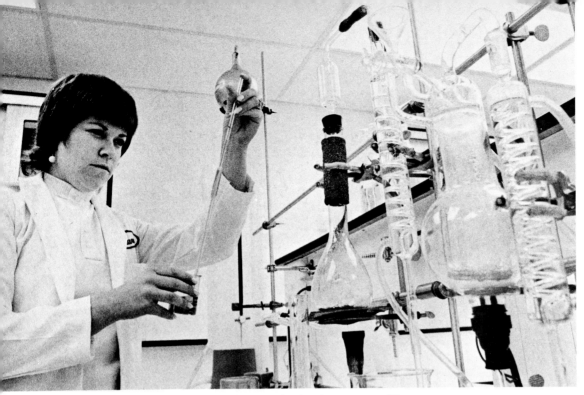

THE ACID TEST. Winery labs analyze each wine for many qualities.

TO BLEND. The Christian Brothers winemaker makes a tiny sample.

THINKING AHEAD. Pedroncelli winemaker tastes for what will be.

Starting in December 🍇

Time of decision

Soon after the tumultuous arrival of new vintage wines, a winemaster must turn his attention to older vintages still in cask. Cellars specializing in varietal reds may have wines in barrels going back four years. Sherry and Port stocks can range back to the 1940s. The cellarmaster must make regular rounds, tasting each lot, deciding to bottle now or wait longer. During the waiting period, each cask must have a monthly topping of wine to replace what is lost to evaporation or tasting. Air in a barrel leads to spoiled wine.

SPECIAL CASES. Cellar full of small barrels at Charles Krug is typical of those where wines of extra promise age.

TOPPER. All barrels must be kept brimful.

THE LONE ARBITER. One pruner governs the quality of next year's crop in a Sonoma County vineyard.

Starting in December

The pause that restores

HEART OF THE ART. Pruners opt for the strong buds.

Starting in December after the leaves have dropped, pruners go into the vineyards to cut away the past season's growth of canes. The job goes on, mostly in soggy misery, through late February. It is vital for two reasons. It helps vines regain strength for the next growing season. More important, pruning determines both the quantity and quality of the next crop. The dormant season is also a prime time for controlling vine pests and diseases.

The Big Picture
Where Californians make wine

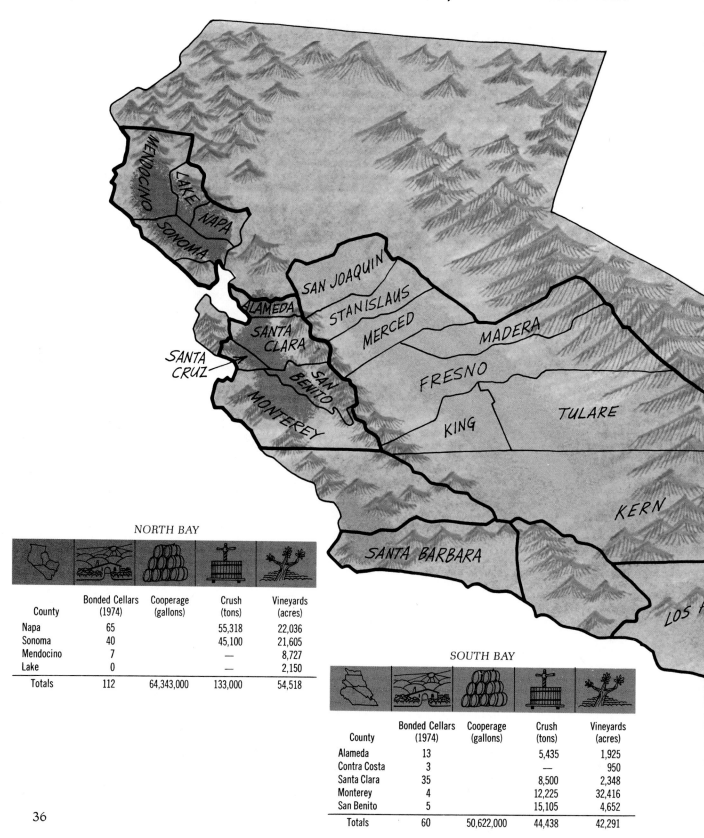

NORTH BAY

County	Bonded Cellars (1974)	Cooperage (gallons)	Crush (tons)	Vineyards (acres)
Napa	65		55,318	22,036
Sonoma	40		45,100	21,605
Mendocino	7		—	8,727
Lake	0		—	2,150
Totals	112	64,343,000	133,000	54,518

SOUTH BAY

County	Bonded Cellars (1974)	Cooperage (gallons)	Crush (tons)	Vineyards (acres)
Alameda	13		5,435	1,925
Contra Costa	3		—	950
Santa Clara	35		8,500	2,348
Monterey	4		12,225	32,416
San Benito	5		15,105	4,652
Totals	60	50,622,000	44,438	42,291

Traditionally, California has been divided into nine geographic districts—
Napa; Sonoma; Alameda-Livermore; Santa Clara-San Benito; Santa Cruz-
Monterey; Lodi; Modesto-Ripon-Escalon; Fresno-Kern; and Cucamonga. In
recent years, however, several of these distinctions have been blurred, or
refocussed. In terms of practical winemaking, the current divisions are—
Napa, Sonoma (which must be linked here as the North Bay region for
statistical reasons, but are in fact distinctly separate); South of San
Francisco Bay; The Great Valley; and the Los Angeles basin.

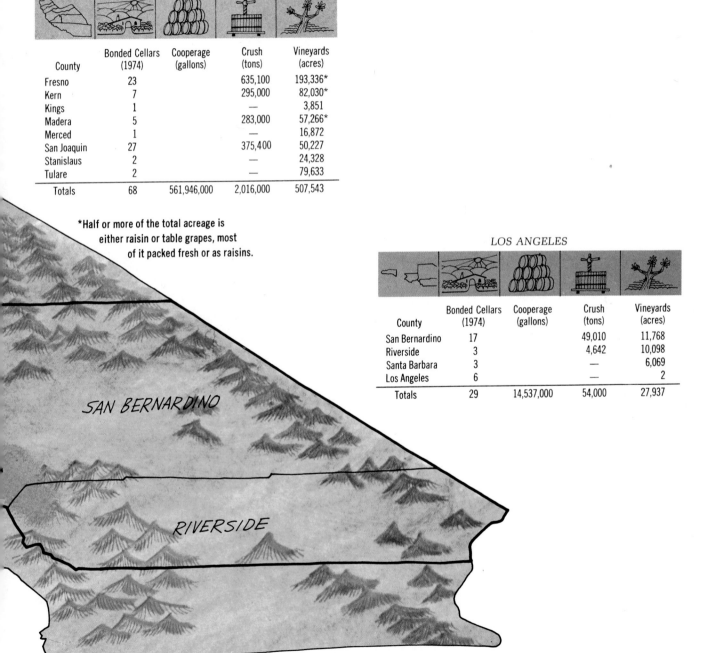

THE GREAT VALLEY

County	Bonded Cellars (1974)	Cooperage (gallons)	Crush (tons)	Vineyards (acres)
Fresno	23		635,100	193,336*
Kern	7		295,000	82,030*
Kings	1		—	3,851
Madera	5		283,000	57,266*
Merced	1		—	16,872
San Joaquin	27		375,400	50,227
Stanislaus	2		—	24,328
Tulare	2		—	79,633
Totals	68	561,946,000	2,016,000	507,543

*Half or more of the total acreage is
either raisin or table grapes, most
of it packed fresh or as raisins.

LOS ANGELES

County	Bonded Cellars (1974)	Cooperage (gallons)	Crush (tons)	Vineyards (acres)
San Bernardino	17		49,010	11,768
Riverside	3		4,642	10,098
Santa Barbara	3		—	6,069
Los Angeles	6		—	2
Totals	29	14,537,000	54,000	27,937

SAN BERNARDINO

RIVERSIDE

GARRETT'S GHOST. The gloomily fine ruins of what used to be a major winery stand at the intersection of old Route 66 and Haven Avenue in Cucamonga. The district is full of ancient invitations and new ones to do something other than make wine. From the vineyardist's point of view, these invitations have been too successful.

Time flies in the Los Angeles Basin. The heart of the vineyards moved three times in two centuries to accommodate an eternally rising tide of population. Now, that same population has all but forgotten how much Southern California wine mattered from the beginnings in the 1770s at least until the end of the 1940s.

The Franciscan fathers planted their first vines at San Diego in 1770, give or take a year. However, before 1780 San Gabriel, east of what is now Los Angeles, became the biggest and best source of mission wine. It retained these twin distinctions until the Mexican government secularized all 21 missions during the 1830s.

By then a French emigrant named Jean-Louis Vignes had gotten wine off to a commercial start. It is more than faintly ironic that his vineyard, the first acknowledged fine one in California, now lies buried beneath a railroad passenger terminal, Union Station, in downtown Los Angeles.

After Vignes' day in the sun ended in the 1860s, the present-day Cucamonga district east of Ontario rose to eminence. For a considerable time it was the biggest single district in the state. It continued to grow until the 1950s, long after San Joaquin Valley districts had surpassed it in vineyard acreage.

At some point between 1900 and 1940, however, the regional climate and soils began to fall between the stools. The North Coast counties around San Francisco Bay were cooler, able to make more elegant table wines. The San Joaquin Valley, as fertile as it was spacious, began to produce more wine of all types at less expense. Then, in the 1950s, as the ever-growing population began to push up land values, times began to be genuinely hard in Cucamonga.

Only a handful of vintners continue in a countryside populated heavily by ghosts, but the survivors seem less haunted than hopeful. In fact, some of them are casting about for new land to plant.

1
Los Angeles
Where it all began

Who makes wine where

Only a few wineries are at present active in the Los Angeles basin and the valleys running eastward from it, the region traditionally known as Cucamonga. This part of California makes good table wines, but the peaks of its reputation are for dessert wines. The grapes for such wines thrive in the long, hot growing season. Whatever the production, most Cucamonga wines can be obtained only within the region.

A tantalizing exception is the Rancho California region, climatically separate, and a developing source of varietal table wines from estate-like wineries.

Aggazzotti Winery—CMA 11919 Foothill Boulevard, Cucamonga 91730
Brookside PO Box 1024, Guasti 91743
Callaway Vineyard & Winery PO Box 275, Temecula 92390
Louis Cherpin 15567 Valley Boulevard, Fontana 92335
J. Filippi PO Box 2, Mira Loma 91752
Galleano 4231 Wineville Road, Mira Loma 91752
Opici 10150 Highland Avenue, Alta Loma 91701
San Antonio 737 Lamar Street, Los Angeles 90031
Thomas-Old Rancho 8916 Foothill Boulevard, Cucamonga 91730

Owing to the urban pressures against vineyard land in the Cucamonga district, much of the future of wine near Los Angeles appears to lie with new vineyard acreages developing in northern Santa Barbara County around the town of Santa Maria, and in southern San Luis Obispo County near Templeton. The two towns are little more than 20 miles apart. Three old-line wineries near Templeton recently have been joined by a pair of newcomers. As the sizeable new vineyards mature, still more wineries are likely to appear.

Firestone Vineyard PO Box 244, Los Olivos 93441
Hoffman Mountain Ranch Adelaida Road, Star Route, Paso Robles 93446
Peseti Route 1, Box 169, Templeton 93465
Rotta Route 1, Box 168, Templeton 93465
York Mountain Route 1, Box 191, Templeton 93465

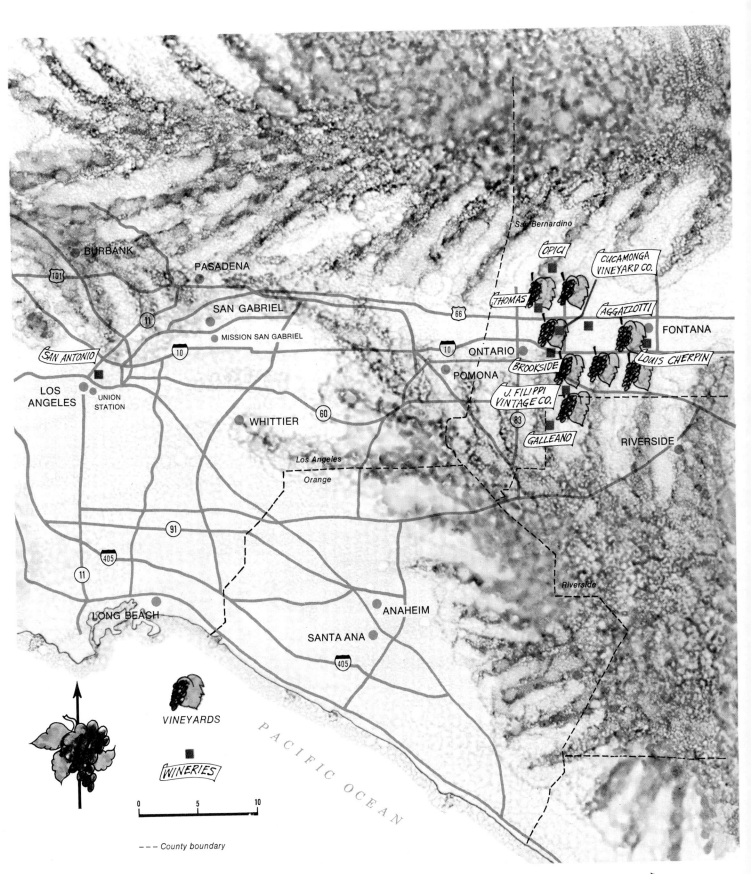

BURBANK

PASADENA

101

SAN GABRIEL

11

MISSION SAN GABRIEL

San Bernardino

OPICI

CUCAMONGA VINEYARD CO.

THOMAS

AGGAZZOTTI

FONTANA

10

ONTARIO

10

BROOKSIDE

LOUIS CHERPIN

SAN ANTONIO

10

LOS
ANGELES

UNION
STATION

POMONA

J. FILIPPI
VINTAGE CO.

83

WHITTIER

60

GALLEANO

RIVERSIDE

Los Angeles

Orange

91

405

Riverside

11

ANAHEIM

LONG BEACH

SANTA ANA

405

VINEYARDS

PACIFIC OCEAN

WINERIES

0   5   10

County boundary

SLIMMER PICKINGS. Workers harvest 13,000 acres each fall within sight of the San Gabriel Mountains. But the total ran upwards of 25,000 as late as the 1950s. Now, Southern Cal-Edison generates energy instead of grapes, and jets land where vines used to grow at Ontario International.

Hanging in there . . .
and still looking good

Although the brightest days have come and gone in the Cucamonga district, it still holds some highly active wineries and some immaculately farmed vineyards. Brookside Vineyard Company, the dominant winery in the early 1970s, crushes well more than half the local crop. Of the 13,000 acres still in vineyard in San Bernardino County, the single most important variety is Zinfandel, with 3,600 acres. Missions still account for 2,505 acres in their ancestral home.

ZINFANDELS. These grapes became Brookside wine.

BIG AS MUSKET BALLS. Mission grapes came with the Franciscans in 1769.

PENNY A POUND. A picker at an independent ranch in Cucamonga hustles his 35-pound pan of grapes to the paymaster.

SOURCE OF THE SOIL. Most of the vineyards in the Cucamonga district are planted in the broad alluvial fan that spreads apronlike at the base of the San Gabriel Mountains.

Epitome of a place

In recent years Brookside Vineyards has come to epitomize winemaking south of the Tehachapi Mountains, in part because the company occupies the greatest of the old winery buildings in Cucamonga, in part because it has grown from the efforts of five generations of one owning family, but mainly because Brookside first found the most effective of the current keys to prosperity in the Los Angeles basin: direct sales from winery to consumer.

Between 1952 and 1972, Philo Biane and his family built a rambling empire of winery-owned tasting rooms-cum-retail stores all over California. With these, Brookside outstripped everybody else whose grapes grow in Cucamonga.

FAMILY TIES. Philo Biane rebuilt Brookside, a label founded by his great uncle, Emile Vaché.

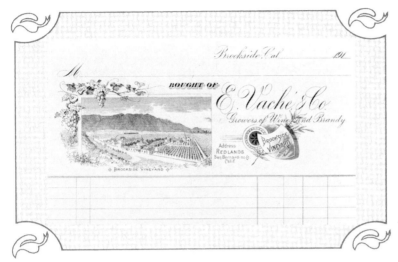

SOURCE OF A NAME. The Brookside label dates from the 1880s, when E. Vaché & Co. made wine alongside a brook in Redlands. Marius Biane worked for Emile Vaché and his brothers, marrying one of the bosses' daughters.

After Prohibition, Marius and his sons, Philo and Francois, revived Brookside at Guasti in a huge winery built to compete with the Vachés back in the 1880s.

Finally, in 1973, the second and third generations of Bianes sold Brookside to a corporation, Beatrice Foods.

SECOND HOME. Brookside occupies the original Italian Vineyard Company cellars, built to compete with E. Vaché.

TASTEFUL WELCOME. Visitors to Opici sample the wines at the only place Opici wines can be bought in California—the source. This pattern, set by Brookside, also holds true for Aggazzotti's CMA, Louis Cherpin, J. Filippi, and the Filippi-owned Thomas Winery. Roadside signs advertising the tasting rooms of these and other wineries dot the district roadsides from Upland to Fontana. Some operate additional tasting rooms in other parts of Southern California.

Signs of
the times

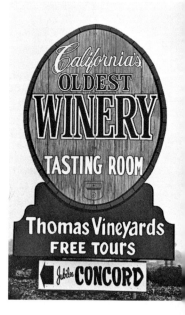

The growing army of ghosts

THE LAST VAI. When Cesare Vai sold the Cucamonga Vineyard Company in the spring of 1973, it marked the departure of yet another old-time Cucamonga district wine family. Before Cesare, James and John Vai ran the winery with great success as Padre Vineyards.

Guidebooks to California wine published in the 1940s and 1950s show a whole host of once-famous names that no longer exist in the world of Southern California wine.

The most recent to go by the boards was Regina, long the property of the Ellena family. Shortly after the Heublein corporation bought the property in 1971, it turned the winery into a full-time vinegar works. Regina joined a ghostly legion that already included Garrett, Italian Vineyard Company, and San Gabriel.

With the mighty have gone the small. Local wineries like A. Filippi, Fountain, and Liabeuf disappeared one after another.

Even in the prosperous 1970s, old names go without calling up replacements. The number of bonded wineries in San Bernardino County has dropped from 25 to 16 since 1964 alone.

The founding Fathers

Both wines and vines came to San Diego from Baja California with Fra Junipero Serra in 1769. By any definition, Serra thus became the first father of California wine—although not the abiding one.

The grape he brought came to be called the Mission. It was either a pure Spanish variety, or else a Spanish vine grafted onto native Mexican roots. In any case, the Mission was the only grape grown by California's Franciscan padres from its introduction at San Diego until the 1830s, when settlers in Los Angeles first added some of the classic European varieties to California's vineyards.

Serra and his colleagues coaxed a surprising variety of wines out of their one grape. Official records indicate that they made a sweet white by fermenting without the skins, both a dry and sweet red by fermenting the juice and skins together, and, finally, a sweet wine fortified by the addition of brandy.

Critical reception was extremely uneven, as was the case with all of California's early wines. Charitable visitors loved them, but these were fewer in number than people who formed low opinions. It would seem that a French visitor to Los Angeles formed the fairest opinion in 1827: the grapes were good, but the frontier winemaking techniques were not.

Undoubtedly there were variations from one mission to the next because of different climates in the vineyards, on the one hand, and better or worse equipment in the cellars on the other.

The long-term contribution of mission vineyards is limited. They proved that grapes could be grown and gave the first hints of the complex microclimates of the coast regions. The Mission variety did not grow at all well in either Santa Clara or Mission San Jose, the coolest climes in which it was planted, but it prospered at Mission San Gabriel, where the production of wine grew to a peak of 50,000 gallons a year.

Mission Winemaking

MISSION VINEYARDS. As the Mission chain developed from south to north over a span of years, one site after another came to its peak development. The following chart lists the largest number of vines at each, all attained within the two decades of the 1830s and 1840s.

Mission	No. of vines
San Gabriel	163,579
San Fernando	32,000
San Buenaventura	11,970
San Jose	11,039
San Diego	5,860
San Juan Bautista	5,200
La Soledad	5,000
San Antonio	4,000
Santa Barbara	3,695
San Rafael	2,000
Santa Cruz	1,210
Sonoma	1,000
Santa Clara	650
San Miguel	166

THE BIGGEST WINERY. In the 1830s the Franciscan missionaries at San Gabriel produced as much as 50,000 gallons of wine a year, the greatest amount made at any mission. Their winery was the 14 by 20-foot building almost hidden by the cross in the mission cemetery. Indians trampled the grapes on the floor; the juice ran into a well at the lowest corner, from where it was scooped into cowhide bags or barrels for fermentation and aging. The mission had 29 acres of vines by modern count, which suggests a sparse yield of 2 to 3 tons per acre.

How the missions made wine

California always has been good for an anachronism, but one of the best came right at the start in the early mission days.

Later on, the Franciscan fathers would have basket presses, barrels and the other equipment that continues in use even today in small country wineries, but a lack of supply lines in the sudden beginning forced many missions to use pre-Christian techniques and pagan labor to make their sacramental wines.

Indians harvested the meagre crop of grapes, probably into woven baskets. Since sharp knives were hard to come by, they used main strength to pull clusters off the vines. Fortunately, the brittle-stemmed Mission variety lent itself to such picking.

At some missions, Indian porters dumped their loads of grapes onto a sloping winery floor. Other Indians then danced to crush the fruit. The juice ran into a well at a low spot, from where it was scooped into fermentors. More often the grapes were dumped onto a platform of loosely laid saplings. Juice from the crushed grapes trickled down through the platform into reservoirs made of cowhides.

Where no barrels could be had, the fermentors were cowhide bags. The hides were coated with pitch and sewn up, hair side in, much as the Spanish bota is made. These bags had to be made new each year to be flexible enough for a seething fermentation to take place without bursting the bag. New wine fumes more than old, whereas old leather is stiffer than new.

The most primitive mission press—whether it was used before fermentation to make a white wine or afterward to make red—resembled a giant nutcracker. The same principle of using a pair of hinged boards to press wine is still commonly followed by amateur winemakers.

There is no indication that the Franciscan fathers kept wine around any longer than they had to. With limited storage facilities and no means of refrigeration or other protection for their wines, they probably were glad to begin each new vintage at the earliest possible moment. Their best wines probably went into barrels, but most went directly from leathern bag to the consumer.

California original: Angelica

Angelica

Meilleur procédé de fabrication pour obtenir un vin qui s'éclaircit rapidement et naturellement.

Le meilleur moût à employer est celui qui pèse 26% de sucre. Si le moût de mission, le seul et meilleur raisin qui doit être employé pour cette fabrication, pèse 28 ou 30%, le ramener à 26% en y ajoutant du moût de Burger.
Le laisser séjourner de 12 à 20 heures, si la température n'est pas trop élevée, dans une cuve ouverte, et le couler ensuite dans les cuves de la fortification en ayant soin de ne pas prendre le chapeau que le liquide a déjà formé.
Le point essentiel est de ne pas laisser fermenter le moût qui doit être employé. En le fortifiant avant que la fermentation se déclare, (Ceci est pourtant contre la loi des Etats Unis), on obtiendra de l'Angelica à 20% d'alcool et 14 p % qui sera parfaitement clair 4 mois après la fabrication. Du moût à 25 p % de sucre donne de l'Angelica à 13 p % de sucre.

WINEMAKER'S RECIPE. In 1891 Emile Vaché wrote out his notes on winemaking. The translation for Angelica:

"Best production procedure for obtaining a wine that clarifies rapidly and naturally.

"The best must to use is one which measures 26% sugar. If the must from Missions—the best grape and the only one that should be used for this product—measures 28 or 30%, bring it back down to 26% by adding some must from Burger. Let [the must] rest in an open tank from 12 to 20 hours, if the temperature is not too high, then run it into the fortifying tanks, taking care not to get any of the cap already formed on the liquid.

"The essential point is not to allow fermentation to start in the must being used. By fortifying before fermentation spoils it (which, for what it is worth, is against United States law), one obtains Angelica of 20% alcohol and 14% sugar. This will be perfectly clear 4 months after its production. A must of 25% sugar yields an Angelica of 13% sugar."

As a name, Angelica is the original California original. The Franciscans made such a wine, although the name may not have been coined until after they had come and gone. In any case it goes back to the early days and pays homage to Los Angeles. As Emile Vaché's reproduced notes indicate, the basic technique was to mix fresh juice from Mission grapes with brandy. The usual proportion was three gallons of juice to one of brandy, the latter running to 180 proof. Made in this way, Angelica is simple and uncommonly sweet. In the early days, its critical reception was mixed at best. However, an 1875 had become a superb old dessert wine by 1968; a surviving bottle proved that. Contemporary Angelicas are made more in the way of sweet Sherry.

BEFORE UNION STATION. In the mid-1800s El Aliso was the largest and finest of a score of vineyards in what is now downtown Los Angeles. El Aliso stood where Union Station stands now.

Vignes, the forgotten father of wine

A largely forgotten man named Jean-Louis Vignes recently has been put forward as a more suitable Father of California Wine than Agoston Haraszthy, who has held the post. Vignes fell into obscurity as a matter of chance. His credentials always have been impeccable. Even his name translates as "vines." But the entire district he helped found disappeared beneath downtown Los Angeles by the turn of the century while Haraszthy's personal estate has survived almost intact through the years.

The fate of his property aside, Vignes was a remarkable force in his day. He came from Cadillac, near Bordeaux, in 1833. Before 1840 his El Aliso Vineyard approached 100 acres. By all accounts he was making more and better wine than any other grower in California. Advertisements of the time list the types as white, red, Port, and Angelica. Most of his wine came from Mission grapes, but some was from varieties he imported from France. He had the patience, unique then, to age his wines for eight and ten years in oak casks coopered from trees on the property. In addition to his own winemaking, he induced a considerable number of his countrymen to emigrate to California, provided nursery stock to other vineyardists from every corner of the state, and established coastwise commerce in wine as far north as San Francisco.

Vignes retired in 1855 and died in 1862 at the age of 83. Nephews named Sainsevain continued El Aliso Vineyards only until 1867. A few years later San Bernardino County began to replace Los Angeles as the premier district south of the Tehachapis.

NO TRACE SURVIVES. F.A. Korn had a typically substantial but short-lived Anaheim winery.

Anaheim, and alas

In 1888, a mysterious vine blight called Pierce's Disease forever put an end to grape growing in Anaheim just three decades after its beginnings. Blessings disguise themselves in odd ways.

The start was brave. In fact, it was Utopian. Forty-six German-Americans banded together to form a cooperative winegrowing colony, the Los Angeles Vineyard Society. They paid $2,000 apiece in 1857 to buy and develop 1,165 acres of barren land six miles south of the Santa Ana River.

Utopia proved as elusive as always. Within two years the hopes for it vanished in spite of a prodigious irrigation achievement. The investors divided the commune equably among themselves and pursued their fortunes individually.

Anaheim wines, almost all from Mission grapes, were not praised, but in a time of critical shortage they sold. By 1872 the colony had 1,200 inhabitants, had doubled its acreage, and was making 600,000 gallons of wine a year.

Pierce's Disease spared Anaheim the test of earnest competition, leaving residents to turn to oranges and walnuts and prosper more than ever.

Palmy days in Cucamonga

From the Gay Nineties through the mid-1940s, the Cucamonga wine district was one of California's best-known, as well as largest. Much of that prosperity was owed to Secundo Guasti, who founded Italian Vineyard Company in 1883 and built it into a 5,000 acre colossus before Prohibition. His was a classic European agricultural estate complete with its own workshops and housing—even its own church. Eventually IVC became too much for one family to handle. Garrett & Co. bought IVC in 1945, ran it for a few years, then sold the estate in several fractions. Brookside preserves the core of the old winery complex as its main cellars.

SECUNDO GUASTI. He built IVC into an empire.

Picking the biggest vineyard

After Prohibition Guasti's brother-in-law, Nicola Giulii, restored IVC. To harvest the 5,000-acre vineyard—largest in the world in its day—his firm used a portable railroad system that foreshadowed today's more flexible gondola system.

THE COOPERAGE. IVC, like all big wineries of its day, had its own workshops.

GRAPE EXPECTATIONS. Brookside vineyard in Long Valley divides its 500 acres among several grape varieties. The white grapes used to make Vertdoux Blanc prosper. A laggard patch in mid-vineyard betrays the unaccountable refusal of Gamay to grow well.

New hope: Rancho California

Winemakers do not give up easily. Recent shrinkage in San Bernardino County vineyards has been offset largely by expansion in the sprawling expanses of Rancho California, 65 miles southeast in Riverside County. Some 1,100 acres of pioneer vineyard dot the rolling hills east of Temecula on US 395. The potential exceeds 10,000 acres, all within reach of irrigation, all washed by sea air flowing through a gap in the coast mountains.

Fittingly, the much-traveled Brookside Vineyard Company is the major owner of vineyards. Just as fittingly, a spanking new, estate-like winery called Callaway makes the greatest point of its location.

Planting began in 1967. All of the classic varieties of *Vitis vinifera* are well represented.

New hope: The central coast

If Los Angeles is to have more than one wine district close to home—creating a counterpart to the happy relationship between San Francisco and the wine valleys ringing San Francisco Bay—the additions are likely to be around Santa Maria in Santa Barbara County, west of Templeton in San Luis Obispo County, or in both places.

Within the wine industry, Santa Barbara County always has been counted as part of the Los Angeles district. Now that vineyard acreage near Santa Maria has shot from a handful of vines in 1959 to 2,000 acres in 1972, this appendix to the district has become an important part of its statistics. However, for lack of existing local wineries, the early crops from Santa Maria vines have gone to established firms as far north as Lodi and Napa.

A LONG ROW TO HOE. In misty sea air, a vineyard crew begins spring cleaning in a new 1,200-acre vineyard of fine varietal grapes near Sisquoc, a few miles east of Santa Maria.

ONLY THE BEGINNING. Benchlands along the Sisquoc River near Santa Maria held more than 2,000 acres of young vines in 1972. The figure will double when tilled soil is planted. Most of this property belongs to a ranching company called Tepusquet.

GOING BACK. Pesenti vineyards near Templeton date back to the 1920s. Grapes have been a part of San Luis Obispo County agriculture since the 1880s. Zinfandel has been the mainstay grape variety.

San Luis Obispo County has fewer vines than Santa Barbara but a long tradition of local winemaking. The 1972 vineyard acreage was 900. Three venerable wineries called Pesenti, Rotta, and York form a close-knit triangle in the hills west of Templeton. Between the 1880s and now, they and their forerunners have demonstrated that the region can make distinctive wines.

LOST CHORD. The legendary pianist Ignace Paderewski admired farming in all of its gentlemanly aspects. He caused a fine vineyard of Zinfandels to be planted as part of his Rancho San Ignacio, six miles west of Paso Robles. Prohibition kept him from doing anything commercial about wine, although one lot (which the York family helped him make) won a state fair gold medal soon after Repeal.

Prohibition and Paderewski departed the land very close together. Now, only a hillside of dead and dying vines and a lug box remain to remind wine fanciers of San Ignacio Zinfandel.

NEIGHBORS. Pesenti and Rotta family members have made wine next door to each other since 1934. The Rotta winery dates back to the 1880s under a previous ownership.

REVITALIZED. The Old York Mountain Winery, after a period of ebbing fortunes, was bought from the founding family in 1971 by a long-time Champagne-maker named Max Goldman. The owner and his son are turning the winery into a Champagne cellar by easy stages from his home base in Los Angeles. The tasting room is already in business, presided over by Pamela Knott and a small circle of friends.

NEW DIRECTIONS. Paul Masson's
1,000-acre vineyard at Soledad
symbolizes a shift of old names to
new places. When urban crowding
made it hard to grow grapes in
Santa Clara and Alameda Counties,
the old wine companies turned south,
consoled to see some developers of
suburban housing pay tribute to the
displaced vines.

The vineyards south of San Francisco Bay stand somewhere near the completion of a revolution of such scope that a latter-day Rip Van Winkle would hardly know where to look for a vine. Twenty years ago, San Benito and Monterey Counties could count scarcely 1,000 acres of grapes between them while Alameda and Santa Clara Counties were famous old winegrowing districts.

Now Monterey and San Benito Counties have a joint acreage surpassing 37,000; Alameda and Santa Clara Counties grow just 4,200 acres of vines between them. Even more striking, wineries that once exemplified Santa Clara on the one hand and Alameda's Livermore Valley on the other now find themselves close neighbors in the new territories. Others have fled to new climes altogether.

In the late 1950s, the three principal wineries in the Livermore Valley were Concannon, Cresta Blanca and Wente Bros. Almaden and Paul Masson were then the dominant names in the Santa Clara district centered on San Jose.

By the late 1960s, Paul Masson and Wente Bros. had become grape-growing neighbors in Monterey County's Salinas Valley. Almaden had shifted most of its vines to Paicines in San Benito County. Cresta Blanca had fled lock, stock, and barrels to Mendocino County. Of the old names, only Concannon Vineyard has stayed where home always has been.

More amazing than the shift, however, is the continuity. When it became obvious that urban growth was an irresistible force and viniculture was not an immovable object, the winemakers began casting around for a union of sun and soil that would yield the kind of wines they had been making all along. It was a highly scientific search that pointed toward the spacious, sparsely settled valleys to the south.

Enough remains of the old to allow comparison with the new.

2

South of San Francisco Bay

Old wine, new space

Who makes wine where

In the sprawling region south of San Francisco Bay the emphasis is on table wines, especially varietals, although the larger producers (especially Almaden and Paul Masson) make all types. Weibel specializes in sparkling wines. These three firms have wineries and vineyards in two or more counties. The others have single cellars.

Livermore/Alameda County

Concannon Vineyards 4590 Tesla Road, Livermore 94550
Villa Armando 553 St. John Street, Pleasanton 94566
Weibel 1250 Stanford Avenue, Mission San Jose 94538
Wente Bros. 5565 Tesla Road, Livermore 94550

Santa Clara County

Almaden 1 Maritime Plaza, San Francisco 94111
Bertero 3920 Hecker Pass Highway, Gilroy 95020
Bonesio-Uvas 11550 Watsonville Road, Gilroy 95020
David Bruce 21439 Bear Creek Road, Los Gatos 95030
Conrotto 1690 Hecker Pass Highway, Gilroy 95020
Filice 2003 El Camino Real, Mountain View 94040
Fortino 4525 Hecker Pass Highway, Gilroy 95020
Gemello 2003 El Camino Real, Mountain View 94040
Emilio Guglielmo 1480 E. Main Avenue, Morgan Hill 95037
Hecker Pass 4605 Hecker Pass Highway, Gilroy 95020
Thomas Kruse 4390 Hecker Pass Highway, Gilroy 95020
Live Oaks 3875 Hecker Pass Highway, Gilroy 95020
Paul Masson 13150 Saratoga Avenue, Saratoga 95070
Mirassou Route 3, Box 344, Aborn Road, San Jose 95121
Mt. Eden 22000 Mt. Eden Road, Saratoga 95070
Nepenthe 216 Corte Madera Road, Portola Valley 94025
Novitiate of Los Gatos PO Box 128, Los Gatos 95030
Pedrizzetti Route 2, Box 166, Morgan Hill 95037
Richert & Sons PO Box 188, Morgan Hill 95037
Ridge 17100 Montebello Road, Cupertino 95014
San Martin PO Box 53, San Martin 95046
Woodside Vineyards 340 Kings Mountain Road, Woodside 94062

Santa Cruz/Monterey Counties

Bargetto 3535 North Main Street, Soquel 95073
Chalone Vineyard PO Box 855, Soledad 93960
Enz Vineyards 1781 Limekiln Road, Hollister 95023
Monterey Peninsula 2999 Monterey-Salinas Highway, Monterey 93940
The Monterey Vineyard 800 S. Alta Street, Gonzales 93926
Turgeon & Lohr 1000 Lenzen Avenue, San Jose 95126

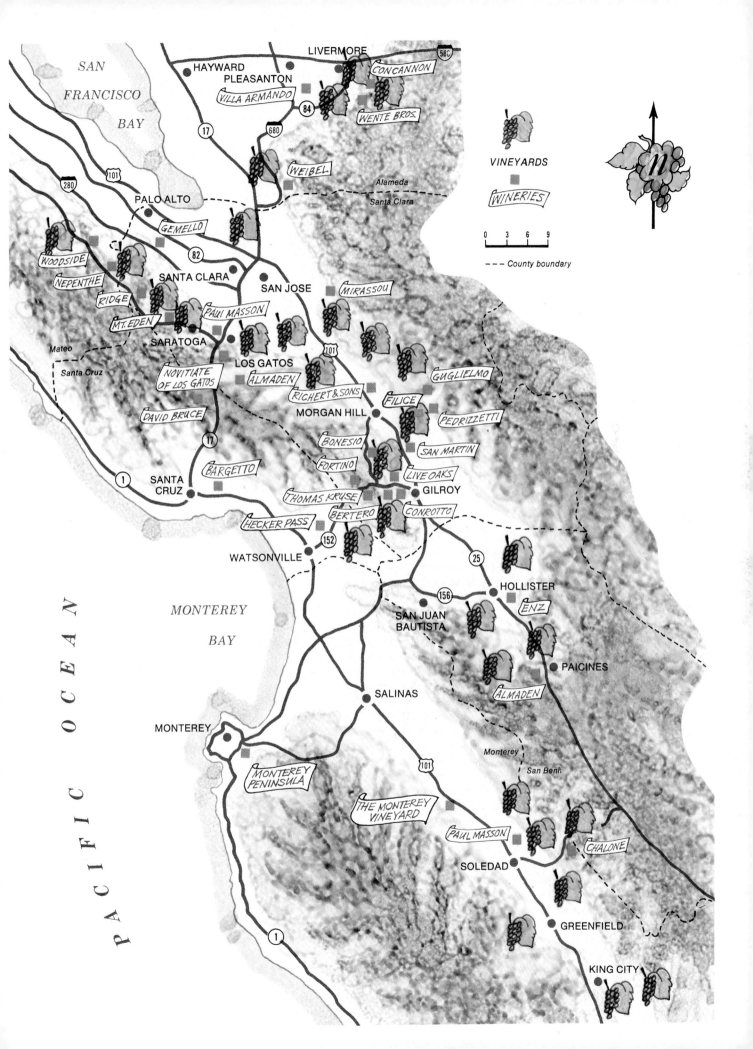

Population: the relentless press

Steady population growth in the San Francisco Bay Area has done away with several thousand acres of vines in Alameda and Santa Clara Counties since the 1940s.

The pressures are more diverse than they would seem.

The main one, of course, is space. As vineyardist Edmund Mirassou ruefully describes the problem: "First, a home is necessary, so the subdivider builds a tract of homes on 1,000 acres. Then come the shopping centers of 20 acres each, along with grade schools of 10 acres for each site and high schools of 40 acres for each site. The space needs for fire stations and other government buildings create additional competing demands for the land and push prices up."

Increased land values mean increased taxes in turn. There is one 40 acre plot in Livermore, for example, that paid $400 in taxes in the 1940s and reached a peak of $5000 in taxes during the 1960s.

Once urban population begins to nibble at the edges of the vineyards, subtler problems set in. To use Livermore as an example again: the water table in the 1940s stood about 20 feet below the surface, well within the reach of the long-rooted grape vine. By the 1960s, however, the table had subsided below 100 feet, which meant that irrigation systems had to be installed and maintained in the vineyards.

Smog burns both leaves and grapes on a vine.

Green belt laws have rescued a good many vineyards in recent years. Without these laws, many vineyardists south of San Francisco Bay would be faced with a choice of losing money on grapes or making fortunes by subdividing.

THE PATTERN. The chart shows the influx of people in Alameda and Santa Clara Counties and the consequent shift of vines south to Monterey and San Benito Counties. The picture would be more striking if 1920 were not a low point for vines because of Prohibition.

County (Sq. Mi.)	1920		1940	
	Population	Acreage in Vineyard	Population	Acreage in Vineyard
ALAMEDA (732)				
SANTA CLARA (1,305)				
MONTEREY (3,330)				
SAN BENITO (1,392)				

= 100,000 persons   = 500 acres

FATE. An abandoned vineyard dies by inches outside the fences of a tract that replaced other vines.

1950		1960		1970	
Population	Acreage in Vineyard	Population	Acreage in Vineyard	Population	1972 Acreage in Vineyard

CALIFORNIANA. New Almaden vines add a touch of green to a venerable ranch just east of Paicines.

New space: Paicines

The spot where Almaden's LaCienega Winery now stands first was planted in 1849 by one Emile Vaché, who did not care to participate in The Gold Rush. Yet the district did not grow beyond one small vineyard until 1958 when Almaden plunged in response to urban pressures against its Santa Clara vineyards. The plunge passed the 4,000 acre mark by 1970, which is to say 2,000,000 vines.

THE FIRST CLUE. Wines came from this LaCienega soil in 1850.

WATER IS THE KEY. Almaden's sprawling domain depends on an irrigation system that uses 4 million feet of pipe to service 92,700 sprinkler heads. There are 2.3 million plants to water at Paicines.

In the long search for suitable places to grow grapes in the coastal mountains of California, Dr. A. J. Winkler of the University of California has walked more miles and taken more temperatures than any other man. He is largely credited with establishing the suitability of the Salinas Valley for commercial vineyards in spite of repeated earlier failures of grapes to grow well in it. The secret of success was in tapping ground water for irrigation of the vines.

LONELY. Tiny Chalone vineyard, just below Pinnacles National Monument, has yielded superior grapes since 1919.

The essential point in finding a new vineyard district is to locate a place where the annual climate cycle produces enough sun heat to ripen grapes for making wine.

The problem is not as easy as it sounds. Each of the classic varieties of *Vitis vinifera* evolved in some specific corner of Europe, bred to more and more finicky preference for local climate conditions.

To get the right grape varieties planted in the right parts of California, Dr. Winkler and his colleagues at the University of California divided the state into five climate zones based on European models ranging from the north of France to the south of Spain. The zones are based on the cumulative average temperatures of the growing season.

Of course there is more to finding good vineyard land than the mere measuring of temperature. Soil and drainage patterns have to fall within defined limits to grow grapes at all. To grow great grapes, land must conform to very real but immeasurable standards. John Daniel, when he owned Inglenook, liked Napa Valley soil that was not quite rich enough to grow commercial prunes. Norman Bundgard, Paul Masson vineyard manager at Soledad, favors benchlands that drain just a little too quickly for lettuce to prosper. Such local signs ultimately provide the keys to the finest vineyard lands.

The hunt for new space

Figuring the weather

In Europe, climate patterns for grapes are mostly a matter of the cool German north, temperate French middle, and hot Spanish south. In California, the coolest areas are coastal valleys affected directly by sea air; the hottest ones are the Great Central Valley and the region south of the Tehachapi Mountains.

To define the California regions, scientists at the University of California set up five climate zones based on cumulative temperatures:

I fewer than 2,500 degree days
II 2,501 to 3,000 degree days
III 3,001 to 3,500 degree days
IV 3,501 to 4,000 degree days
V more than 4,001 degree days

The cumulative figures are the sum of daily figures for the growing season, April 1 through October 31. The daily figure is the difference between the average temperature and 50°F.

Taking a hypothetical April 1:
High 76, Low 42; Average 59; Degree Days 9
(76 + 42 = 118 ÷ 2 = 59 − 50 = 9)

With both the quality of fruit and the economics of growing it in mind, the university recommends planting grapes according to the climate zones. (HR is highly recommended; R is recommended;

QR is qualified recommendation; NR is not recommended.)

Examples, with their European districts of origin, show the progression from cool to warm.

ZONE	I	II	III	IV	V
(Varieties from Germany or Alsace)					
Gewurztraminer	R	QR	NR	NR	NR
White Riesling	HR	R	NR	NR	NR
(Varieties from Burgundy)					
Chardonnay	HR	R	NR	NR	NR
Pinot Noir	R	QR	NR	NR	NR
(Varieties from Bordeaux)					
Sauvignon Blanc	HR	R	R	NR	NR
Semillon	QR	R	R	QR	NR
Cabernet Sauvignon	HR	R	QR	NR	NR
(Varieties from Italy)					
Moscato Canelli	QR	R	R	NR	NR
Barbera	NR	QR	R	R	QR
(Varieties from Spain or Portugal)					
Palomino	NR	NR	NR	QR	R
Tinta Madeira	NR	QR	QR	R	HR

NEVER GIVE A SUCKER AN EVEN BREAK. At Soledad, a crew removes sucker canes from Masson vines.

New space:
Salinas Valley

ARTIFICIAL RAIN. Overhead mist irrigation doubles the 10 inches of natural rain at Wente's Arroyo Seco ranch.

On the benchlands from Gonzales southward to King City, vineyards prosper in the Salinas Valley, otherwise known as the lettuce capital of the world.

This is the supreme testimonial in California to date that scientific research can uncover new vineyard districts. From no acres of grapes at all in 1961, the region rushed to 13,000 acres in vines in 1972, then 37,000 acres in 1975. The pioneer owners were Paul Masson, Mirassou and Wente Bros. Much new blood has come since, notably The Monterey Vineyard and San Martin.

The cool, misty north end of the valley is devoted mostly to white grapes. In the middle, around Greenfield, both white and red varieties do well. Toward the southerly end, even sherry-types will grow.

TEAMWORK. At a Mirassou Vineyards ranch, the mechanical harvesters are rigged with crushers. New must flows continuously into a tank pulled down an adjacent row. Stems stay in the vine rows.

Hey, that thing picks pretty good

In the Salinas Valley a small vineyard runs upwards of 200 acres. A big one touches 1,000. Size, gentle terrain, and new plantings all combined to make this an ideal environment for mechanical harvesters.

Although it pains purists to think so, the big machines may end up doing a better job than human hands. Already, mechanical picking gets grapes from vines to fermentors far faster than hand picking does, to the benefit of the wine. A crew of three can machine-pick an acre in a bit less than an hour. Three hand pickers can cover no more than a sixth of an acre in the same time.

To date, harvesters rigged to crush grapes right in the vineyard produce better wine than those that only pick, leaving the crushing until later. Only more years of experience will give answers to some of the long range effects, 1970 being the first year in which machines harvested grapes commercially.

MILE RELAY. Tractor-tank combinations must work in relays to keep pace with a mechanical harvester. When one tank fills, a second moves into place, and the parade keeps rolling.

How mechanical harvesters do it

Mechanical harvesters pick grapes one at a time rather than by clusters. Oscillating batons shake the vines hard enough to make the berries fall off. They drop onto conveyor belts that carry the fruit either into a gondola running in an adjoining row or into a crusher mounted on the harvester. Crushed fruit is pumped into a tank running alongside the harvester. Full tanks or gondolas are driven to the winery.

AND THE RAINS CAME. Autumn clouds bump and scrape across David Bruce's mountain-top vineyard.

VOLUNTEERS. Friends of Thomas Kruse begin to pick his Gilroy vines.

Meanwhile: back in Santa Clara

Vineyards in Santa Clara County have dwindled from
a peak of 8,000 acres to just 2,000, yet the district
has lost not a jot of its legendary diversity.

No other county in California ever has harbored
such a disparity of winegrowers as this one still does.
David Bruce and his $27-a-bottle Chardonnay coexist
peaceably with Pete Scagliotti and his $1.50 Vin Rosé.
Between, every shade and hue of wine can be had
at whatever price one wishes to pay.

In the main, the differences owe themselves to
climate. The north end of the county is cooled—more
here, less there—by air flowing across it from
ocean to bay, which has led to the planting of such
elegant grape varieties as Cabernet Sauvignon,
Pinot Noir, and Chardonnay. The south end is not
blessed by the same natural cooling. As a
result, its vineyards hold Chasselas, Grenache, and
Zinfandel, grapes that lend themselves to wines made in
the country style and bottled in jugs.

The cooling sea air has been a double-edged sword.
While the south county is just beginning to lose
acreage to urbanization, the elegantly cool vineyards of
the north county have long since been decimated
by people seeking an ideal environment for themselves.

VINTAGE 1972. Every year brings a vintage, for better or worse. Sometimes it goes both ways.

The big names in Santa Clara

CONTRADICTIONS. Outside, Paul Masson's Saratoga winery is modern. Inside is an engrossing mixture of the oldest and newest equipment used to make wine.

SANTA CLARA UNDERGROUND. At Novitiate of Los Gatos, ancient oak casks fill several cellars.

The commercial mainstays of winemaking in northern Santa Clara County number just four: Almaden, Paul Masson, Mirassou Vineyards, and The Novitiate of Los Gatos. Although diverse in size and emphasis, the four share long histories and stubborn insistence on keeping their headquarters at ancestral sites. As a result, the winery buildings are approached through rows of houses rather than vines. The grapes from distant vineyards are either crushed at supplementary wineries, or are trucked to the home premises to be made into wine.

THE BIRTHPLACE. The old Charles LeFranc estate in Los Gatos is currently the bottling cellars for Almaden. The winery is flanked by a small patch of vines, then ringed by houses.

ANCIENT ART. Riddling—the hand-turning of Champagne bottles to jostle yeast sediment into the necks for removal—is still a part of the cellar practices at Mirassou Vineyards.

A MATTER OF TASTE. In a carefully designed room, the winemaster and his assistants at Paul Masson taste and retaste each lot of wine during its life in the cellar.

LEARNING NEW TRICKS. Some of the most old-fashioned of California's winemakers use some of the newest tricks in the world of wine to get what they want from their grapes. Max Huebner, in his 70s, oversees what happens in the stainless steel fermenting tanks at Mirassou Vineyards. Visitors can take a first-hand look at the equipment.

ROLLING STOCKS. As late as 1913, California wines were not only made in redwood tanks, but went to market in redwood tanks mounted on trucks and railroad cars. The third generation of the Mirassou family is represented in this photo by Pierre, in the driver's seat. The fourth generation, in the small form of Norbert, rode shotgun.

The currently familiar names in Santa Clara winemaking began to appear in the 1850s, when Pierre Pellier and Charles LeFranc established their first vineyards and wineries in the region.

Pellier's winery became the Mirassou vineyards and winery after his daughter married the first Mirassou, also named Pierre. Now the fourth and fifth generations of Mirassous tend the family business.

LeFranc's winery is the common ancestor of both Almaden and Paul Masson. LeFranc's daughter married a man named Etienne Thee, then one of their daughters married Paul Masson. Some time later Masson established his 100-acre aerie in the hills west of Saratoga as a separate property. Later still he sold the old LeFranc-Thee-Masson property, which became Almaden. Both labels have long since outstripped their original premises under corporate ownerships.

A LA RECHERCHE. Paul Masson revisited his native France from time to time. Wherever he went, the pose was typical.

Of the pre-Prohibition winegrowers, Paul Masson gave Santa Clara County as much flavor and reputation as any.

Masson also had the Frenchman's flair for succinct comment. Among other things, he is alleged to have said . . .

To a fellow clubman in San Jose: "What do you mean, 'Fine wine is wasted in cooking?' Aren't you going to eat it?"

To another clubman who planned to have Sherry before dinner: "The palate was not made for such punishment."

To a fellow winegrower to whose home Masson took his own wines for dinner: "When you make a wine as good as mine, then I'll drink yours."

Mountaintop miniaturists

Somehow the west hills of Santa Clara County have become a grail for a certain kind of winemaker, one willing to lavish care on a 37-gallon lot of Pinot Noir just to see what will come of it.

A man named Martin Ray started the trend in the 1940s when he sold Paul Masson Vineyards to the Seagrams distilling companies and relocated himself as high up as he could get on a ridge west of Saratoga. From that beginning has grown a cluster of half a dozen tiny wineries.

Wines grown here range up to $37 for a new bottle, part of the price reflecting pride and part of it the economics of making very small amounts of wine in a tough place.

THE WHOLE OF IT. Woodside Vineyards winery fits in its entirety beneath the family carport of its owners, Bob and Polly Mullen. The aging capacity is 3,000 gallons, enough for the grapes that come from five vineyards totalling 7 acres. Woodside ranks in the middle of the miniaturists for size. David Bruce and Ridge are several times larger. Nepenthe and Sherill Cellars are slightly smaller.

THE CRUSH. One small crusher operated by friends and neighbors was enough to handle the vintage of 1972 at Mt. Eden Vineyards. Twenty acres of vines yielded twenty tons of grapes.

PRESSING PINOT NOIR. Dr. David Bruce combines modern equipment with ancient methods to make wine at his property west of Saratoga.

BIG AS THEY COME. Ridge Vineyards keeps close to a third of its aging wines in this corner of the old Montebello Wine Cellars west of Cupertino. It is one of the largest of these hill wineries.

Brinksmanship in the vineyards

The tumultuous slopes above Saratoga and Sunnyvale impose severe limits on vineyardists. There are only a few small patches with soil deep enough to hold vines, and those are extraordinarily hard to work. However, this fingertip grip on survival seems to be an important part of the allure for those who would test their wills here.

ECHO OF THE STRUGGLE. In 1894, Dr. Ozea Perone terraced his Montebello Vineyards into the ridge west of Cupertino that still bears their name. The terrain defeated its cultivators even before Prohibition.

HIDDEN BEAUTY. Most of the
vineyards near Gilroy tuck themselves
into folds in the hills away from main
roads. These vines flank Day Road,
northwest of town, the main quarter
for grapes.

NEW FACE. Ernest Fortino is one of
the newcomers who is turning the
Hecker Pass toward varietal wines
rather than country jugs. He bought
the old Cassa Bros. winery in 1969.

In Gilroy, country cousins

Country wine comes not so much from a certain kind of grapes as from a certain state of mind.

People who make country wine intend for it to resemble as much as possible a good jug of home-made wine. Ideally, the resemblance covers both flavor and price.

The last real bastion of such wine in California has its focal point along the Hecker Pass Highway just west of Gilroy in south Santa Clara County. Jugs of thick red wine still go out of old family wineries on the shoulders of regulars who learned the way at the heels of their fathers.

Even here, though, the devotion to an inexpensive jug of country red is giving ground to pricier bottles of varietal wine. Mostly it is made by new names in town, but more than a little is produced by old pillars of the community.

PREMIER KRUSE. Amid all the old Italian families, a Chicago boy, Thomas Kruse, has brought a new name to the Hecker Pass country. He harvests with crews of friends and neighbors.

... In Gilroy, country cousins

THE OLD HANDS. These men are the currently active branches of the old-line families that made Hecker Pass wine what it is. The Angelo Berteros Sr. and Jr. (top) operate the winery that bears their family name. It was founded in 1919. Louis Bonesio (above) holds the reins of his family's Uvas Winery, founded in 1916. Peter Scagliotti (right) is the proprietor of Live Oaks, which was the first of them all in 1912.

A CUP THAT CHEERS. Convivial tasting rooms are a hallmark on the Hecker Pass. Few of the patrons at Scagliotti's Live Oaks winery need to learn how the wine tastes after years of regular visits, but the visit over a glass is unbreakable ritual.

NOTICE
MINORS MAY NOT APPROACH THE BAR. PARENTS NOT ALLOWED TO SERVE THEIR CHILDREN.
CALIF. STATE LAW

Meanwhile: back in Mission San Jose

At this point, one winery surrounded by one small vineyard is all that remains of a district that was sizeable before Prohibition. The lone survivor in Mission San Jose, Weibel, has hedged its bets with a new winery and vineyards in Mendocino County.

Around the turn of the century, the property now occupied by the Weibel family was a major winery under the proprietorship of Senator Leland Stanford and his brother Josiah. The list of local competitors ran long, notably including a prestigious winery called Los Amigos and a big one, the Gallegos Wine Company. In 1906, The Earthquake shook down Gallegos' building. Shortly thereafter, Prohibition dealt the district a blow from which it could never recover.

Although Mission San Jose's vineyards fell within the boundaries of Alameda County, connoisseurs always thought of it as a natural extension of the Evergreen district east of San Jose and prized it for claretlike red wines.

THE HOLDOUT. Weibel Champagne Cellars nestles into vine rows at the foot of Mission Peak.

SHAKEDOWN VICTIM. Juan Gallegos, holder of the Spanish land grant at Mission San Jose, built a three-story winery into a sidehill in the 1880s. But brick walls were the wrong kind to have in the spring of 1906. The Great Earthquake destroyed the building and the business.

VINTAGE OF '98. Pickers harvested Leland Stanford's vineyards in Mission San Jose precisely where the Weibels grow Chardonnay and Pinot noir today.

Meanwhile: back in Livermore

Wine has an eternal fascination for people who like to know that the Davids of the world can prosper even when the Goliaths stalk. One of California's cherished Davids is the Livermore Valley, a place important out of all proportion to its size since the 1880s.

In that early era it was home to Charles Wetmore, the founder of Cresta Blanca and one of the two or three most powerful voices in the California wine industry. Wetmore used his booming voice on behalf of planting ever finer grape varieties and enacting ever stricter regulations to assure fine quality in the state's wines. He set a proper example with his own firm.

In Wetmore's time, Livermore wines made from Sauvignon Blanc and Semillon grapes fared very well at international competitions. After Prohibition, the first California wine to win unstinting praise from a French critic was the Pinot Chardonnay from Wente Bros. By then Herman Wente was the sort of voice Wetmore had been.

The Livermore Valley's lofty reputation is built upon a meager 2,000 acres of vineyard, most of it in white wine varieties, all of it planted in the rocky courses of ancient arroyos south of Livermore town.

When Wetmore was just getting into stride, 2,000 acres of vineyard supported at least a score of wineries. Most have disappeared, leaving little or no trace.

At present, Concannon Vineyard and Wente Bros. own more than half of the valley's vineyards. Some of the old Cresta Blanca vines and buildings endure, although Wetmore's winery has been shut down for years. (The label now operates under other ownership from a base in Mendocino County.) The old Ruby Hill estate is intact but no longer making wine. Villa Armando is a new firm housed in what used to be the Garatti winery in Pleasanton. There are no others.

As owners of the principal wineries, even the Concannon and Wente families admit fears for the future of winegrowing in Livermore. The vineyards are profitable for the moment only because a green belt law keeps the property taxes on them below prevailing rates.

CRESTA BLANCA. Charles Wetmore's old vines still grow in the curving bed of an arroyo.

NEIGHBORS. The old brick facade of Concannon Vineyards and the new face of Wente Bros. are only a few hundred yards apart on opposite sides of Tesla Road near Livermore.

NO STONE UNTURNED. Joe Concannon is the third generation of his family to farm this vineyard.

A rocky existence

The overwhelming fact of life for vineyardists in Livermore is rocky ground. All of the valley's vines grow in a stone-filled wash that runs 600 feet deep. Tilling the vineyards reduces the lifespan of tools to a quarter of normal in the best of conditions, to a tenth in the worst. But Livermore winemakers feel this stony soil makes wine grown in it distinctive from the wine of other districts. The Concannon and Wente families have been working their vineyards since 1881. When they have planted in other districts it has been in the rockiest soils they could find.

TASTE OF THE SOIL. Karl and Ernest Wente taste a Grey Riesling from their Livermore vineyards. (Karl is too young to appear in the photo below, but his father, Ernest, was on hand for both.)

JAMES CONCANNON   THE WENTES, 1894. Ernest is at the left.

A little corner of Bordeaux

LOUIS MEL

MONT ROUGE. One of the famous French-owned wineries in Livermore belonged to the firm of Chauche & Bon. It closed in 1919.

As usual, there is an ironic twist. In the case of Livermore, it is that the district started out to be a little corner of Bordeaux. Before Prohibition, Frenchmen dominated wine-growing there, having been attracted by the similarity of its rocky soil to that of Graves, near Bordeaux. A. G. Chauche and Jules Morier dropped out during Prohibition. Alexander Duval, the proud proprietor of Chateau Bellevue, had already disappeared by then, broken when his daughter ran off with her tutor (proving once again that a little education is a dangerous thing). Louis Mel was the last to go when he retired in the late 1930s — and the most lasting contributor. (Mel had obtained cuttings of Sauvignon blanc and Semillon from Chateau d'Yquem, thereby helping to fix Livermore's reputation for white wine.)

There is not a trace of the old wineries built by French winemakers. The most tangible souvenir is Mel's El Mocho vineyard.

At a winery snugged into a hillside, grapes could arrive at a door on the high side and wine could depart from a door on the low side, having been moved through the fermenting and aging processes by gravity.
When a man had to pump by hand, he moved a quart per stroke. A good man could keep a steady rate of 8 or 9 gallons a minute.
Most early wineries snugged into hillsides. Cresta Blanca did not, to the probable regret of this 1890's cellar worker.

EL MOCHO. Louis Mel's old vineyards, still bearing some old d'Yquem vines, belong to Wente Bros.

ALWAYS SOMETHING NEW. Souverain
Cellars built a showcase winery near
the town of Healdsburg in 1972-1973,
with the announced goal of making
wines that would reveal the many
micro-climates of the Russian River
watershed. 116 years earlier, Agoston
Haraszthy began a similar exploration
of the Sonoma Valley. He built Buena Vista.
The winery continues active today in the
sturdy stone cellars of the founder.

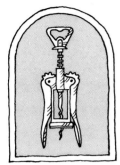

Perhaps because Agoston Haraszthy set the tone, Sonoma County always has attracted winemakers willing to try something new.

Haraszthy was many things . . . a Hungarian revolutionary, a sheriff of San Diego, an official of the U.S. Mint in San Francisco . . . but he was above all an aggressive promoter. One of the things he promoted was the Buena Vista Vinicultural Society, in 1855, in Sonoma town. Once he and his partners had their winery going, Haraszthy promoted the first grand-scale importation of cuttings from great European vineyards, in 1861.

Like other fiery promoters before and since, Haraszthy was made unwelcome in his own enterprise when cooler heads began to work the balance sheets. When he went off to other promotable territories in 1868, Haraszthy left a handsome legacy of 300 fine grape varieties, the notion that Sonoma was amenable to unusual business organizations, and the conviction that its soils would grow whatever type of wine a man wished to attempt. All three contributions have been important to Sonoma wine.

Contemporary Sonoma is at least two separate wine-growing districts. One is the Valley of the Moon. The other is the Russian River Valley.

The Valley of the Moon looks straight into San Francisco Bay, or over one shoulder into the Napa Valley. Most of its vineyards circle the ancient pueblo town of Sonoma, but a sizeable skein stretches north-ward through narrowing hills toward Santa Rosa.

The Russian River Valley is a long and winding water-shed reaching from the Pacific Ocean well up into the interior of Mendocino County, Sonoma's neighbor to the north. A network of tributary valleys add complica-tions that may cause the whole to dissolve into four parts as the vineyardists sort out more and more of the local differences. All of Sonoma has been curiously modest since Prohibition, devoted mainly to making bulk wines. The Russian River, having straggled longest, is now hurrying the fastest to regain its old identity.

3
Sonoma County
A place for new ideas

Who makes wine where

The wineries of Sonoma County long have been a source of inexpensive generic table wines and also a source of wines in bulk for producers in other districts. In recent years there has been a steady evolution toward making and selling varietal table wines. For lack of size, Mendocino has been historically an appendix to Sonoma. It, too, is gaining identity for varietal wines. (North of Sonoma, Mendocino County is not shown on the map, but the labels of its wines are included on this page.)

Russian River Valley

Bynum 8075 Westside Road, Healdsburg 95448
Cambiaso 1141 Grant Avenue, Healdsburg 95448
Dry Creek PO Box T, Healdsburg 95448
Foppiano Vineyards 12781 Old Redwood Highway, Healdsburg 95448
Geyser Peak (Voltaire) Old Redwood Highway North, Geyserville 95441
Italian Swiss Colony c/o United Vintners, 601 Fourth Street, San Francisco 94107
Johnson's 8333 Highway 128, Healdsburg 95448
Korbel Guerneville 95446
Martini & Prati 2191 Laguna Road, Santa Rosa 95401
Pastori 23189 Redwood Highway, Cloverdale 95425
J. Pedroncelli 1220 Canyon Road, Geyserville 95441
Rege 1609 Powell Street, San Francisco 94133
Russian River 98 Post Street, San Francisco 94104
Simi PO Box 946, Healdsburg 95448
Sonoma Vineyards PO Box 57, Windsor 95429
Souverain of Alexander Valley PO Box 528, Geyserville 95441
J. Swan 2916 Laguna Road, Forestville 95436
Trentadue 19170 Redwood Highway, Geyserville 95441

Valley of the Moon

Buena Vista PO Box 500, Sonoma 95476
Chateau St. Jean PO Box 293, Kenwood 95452
Grand Cru 1 Vintage Lane, Glen Ellen 95442
Hacienda 1000 Vineyard Lane, Sonoma 95476
Hanzell 18596 Lomita Avenue, Sonoma 95476
Kenwood PO Box 447, Kenwood 95452
Sebastiani PO Box AA, Sonoma 95476
Valley of the Moon 777 Madrone Road, Glen Ellen 95442
Z-D PO Box 900, Sonoma 95476

Mendocino

Cresta Blanca 1 Jackson Place, San Francisco 94111
Edmeades 5500 State Route 128, Philo 95466
Fetzer 1150 Bel Arbres Road, Redwood Valley 95470
Husch Vineyards PO Box 144, Philo 95466
Parducci Route 2, Box 572, Ukiah 95482

VINEYARDS

WINERIES

0 1 2 3

--- County boundary

Mendocino
Sonoma

CLOVERDALE

101

REGE

ITALIAN SWISS COLONY

AST

GEYSER PEAK *PASTORI*

PEDRONCELLI

GEYSERVILLE

TRENTADUE

128

SOUVERIAN

SIMI

DRY CREEK

HEALDSBURG

JOHNSON

CAMBIASO

FOPPIANO

SONOMA VINEYARD

River

Lake

128

Sonoma

BYNUM

Russian

RIO NIDO

KORBEL

101

Napa

GUERNEVILLE

J. SWAN

MARTINI & PRATI

CH. ST. JEAN

RUSSIAN RIVER

116

12

SANTA ROSA

12

KENWOOD

KENWOOD

GRAND CRU

SEBASTOPOL

GLEN ELLEN

BODEGA BAY

HACIENDA

VALLEY OF THE MOON

HANZELL *BUENA VISTA*

SONOMA

SEBASTIANI

Sonoma

Marin

101

Z-D

PETALUMA

121

PACIFIC OCEAN

ROLLING HOME. Sonoma is not one deep valley, but many shallow ones. Vineyards roll across 17,000 acres of the gentle landscape.

GRAYBEARDS. It is possible, though beyond verification, that some of Buena Vista's Zinfandel vines are originals, planted by the Haraszthys in the 1860s to 1880s.

EARLY TIMES. The wooden sheds are gone. So are the Chinese vineyard workers. Otherwise, Buena Vista looks now much as it did when this photograph was made in 1881.

LONG GONE. Agoston Haraszthy built himself a Pompeiian villa just across the vineyards from his wineries. The elegant structure outlasted him, but burned down many years ago.

Haraszthy's contributions

For a long time Agoston Haraszthy held the undisputed title of Father of California Wine. In recent years, doubts have been put forward about the validity of his claim, but he was the right man in the right place at the right time for making a dramatic impression.

As the founder of the Buena Vista Vinicultural Society, he traveled to Europe on an official mission to acquire cuttings of fine grape varieties from Germany, France, and Italy.

From the resulting nursery stocks came extensive vineyards of his own, and for dozens of other growers throughout the North Coast Counties. Among the varieties was Zinfandel, its origins clouded when tags on the plants became illegible during the sea voyage around Cape Horn.

Thus, in one stroke, Haraszthy turned the North Coast away from Mission grapes, and launched the use of varietal names on California wine.

His old estate continues active today under his name, in his buildings.

The beginning of bubbles

OLD-STYLE CHAMPAGNE. In the 1870s, Buena Vista finished its champagne beneath the winter sun.

The first sustained struggle to make sparkling wine in California came at Buena Vista, where Agoston Haraszthy's son Arpad devoted years to perfecting a Champagne he called Eclipse. Arpad coined the name as fair warning that he meant to put the rest of the world's sparkling wines in the shade. He did not succeed.

However, three Czech brothers named Korbel surpassed his example, in time making sparkling wines that earned much of California's international reputation for the type.

The old brick winery is now owned by the brothers Heck, who continue to make Korbel Champagne but who have added other wines to the long-time specialty.

ARPAD HARASZTHY

THE KORBELS. From left to right, Joseph, Anton, and Francis Korbel pose for an 1880s photographer. They settled on the Russian River to grow tobacco but quickly shifted to Champagne.

TIMELESS OPERATION. The sequence of steps in which Champagne is finished remains just as shown in this 1884 photo at Korbel. Some lines even look much like this one, although larger and more modern machines are now in use at the modernized Korbel winery at Rio Nido.

Getting the bubbles into Champagne

Sparkling wine dates back to the early 1700 s when a French monk named Dom Perignon accidentally stoppered bottles of wine that had not quite finished fermenting.

Prosaic as it may seem, bubbles (CO_2) are a natural by-product of fermentation. In the modern "methode Champenoise," a measured amount of yeast and grape syrup goes into a tank of new wine, which is then bottled and capped. The festive bubbles come from a second fermentation within the sealed bottles.

1. Tirage is the period during which fermentation takes place in the bottle. This goes forward quickly. Depending on how strongly yeast is to flavor the finished wine, the bottle remains on tirage for a few months, or several years.

2. Riddling comes when the winemaker judges the wine ready for drinking. This is the act of moving the bottle from flat to vertical, to coax spent yeasts down into the neck. Every day for weeks a riddler jostles and turns each bottle.

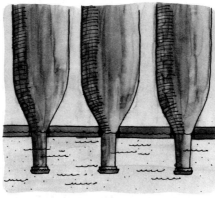

3. When the yeast is settled inside the cap of the upside down bottles, cellarmen place them in a tank holding a shallow 0° brine solution. This freezes a plug of wine inside the neck; the yeast is trapped in the ice.

4. Disgorging removes the yeast. A cellarman pries the crown cap off each bottle. The plug of ice explodes out of the open neck and into a cutaway barrel, carrying the sediment with it. A quick thumb keeps much CO_2 or wine from escaping.

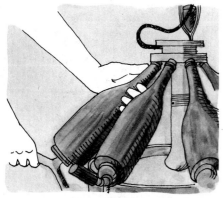

5. Dosage comes next. As soon as the amount of wine lost at disgorging has been replaced, a precisely measured syrup de dosage (brandy and sugar) is added to each bottle. This governs the final degree of sweetness in the Champagne.

6. Recorking follows dosage. The laminated cork is shaped into the familiar mushroom as it is emplaced, then wired in against the CO_2 pressure by complex machines. (Plastic stoppers shaped in advance go in more simply.)

7. After the bottle has been dressed with foil and labels, it is packed into a case and given a brief rest before going to market. This time is mainly to allow the wine to regain its equilibrium after the shakings of disgorgement.

BIT OF BOHEMIA. A brick tower echoes buildings in the Korbel homeland.

OLD FACE, NEW PLACE. The Korbel winery now holds some ingenious improvements on traditional champagne equipment. For example, a wizard machine now does the riddling.

FOUNTAINGROVE. The winery—now dismantled—was on hills just north of Santa Rosa.

Once upon a time ... Utopia

Two famous Utopian wineries sprang up in nineteenth century Sonoma. Fountaingrove began in 1882 as an adjunct to a religious cult. Italian Swiss Colony started in 1881 as a cooperative commune. Both helped to prove that Utopia is harder to make than good wine.

Theologically speaking, Thomas Lake Harris' Brotherhood of the New Life ranked among the odder of California's religious cults, but its Fountaingrove Winery at Santa Rosa was orthodox and highly regarded. After Harris disproved his basic belief by dying, the Brotherhood disbanded, leaving cellarmaster Kanaye Nagasawa as proprietor of the winery. He and his wines became legends. Without him, Fountaingrove could manage no more than a brief, tottery revival after Prohibition.

Italian Swiss Colony was founded by Andrea Sbarbaro as a self-help commune for Italian Swiss made destitute in San Francisco by the great depression of that era. Utopia did not even begin to blossom, so Sbarbaro smoothly reorganized ISC into a conventional company. The label has been a major factor in California wine ever since.

ITALIAN SWISS. Founder Andrea Sbarbaro built Italian Swiss Colony into a major winery between 1888 and 1919. Sbarbaro died in 1923, but after Prohibition his winemakers—Edmund and Robert Rossi—revived the business. United Vintners-Heublein is the most recent of several subsequent owners. A third generation of Rossis still makes wine at the big winery near Cloverdale. Sbarbaro's old mansion still graces the grounds.

STATEMENT OF INTENT. Hanzell was modeled on a façade of the Clos de Vougeot in Burgundy. The winery and vineyards now belong to Barbara de Brye.

Where barrels come from

Today, aging cellars in North Coast wineries still hold American white oak and redwood cooperage as always, but many also hold barrels from one or several parts of Europe, especially Germany, Yugoslavia, and France. Winemakers taste for the effects of differing kinds of wood on their wine as carefully as consumers taste to find favorite bottlings. Their decisions are visible as coopers' marks on the heads of many barrels.

A word about wood

REVOLUTIONARY. The late J. D. Zellerbach changed California wine with new barrels.

The late James D. Zellerbach built his Hanzell winery in 1956 to prove or disprove a thought that had long haunted him: that the barrel a wine ages in has a good deal to do with how the wine finally tastes.

A lifelong admirer of great Burgundies, Zellerbach chose to grow Burgundian grapes in California soil, then age the wines in barrels from the French oak forest at Limousin. Burgundians habitually age wines from Pinot noir and Chardonnay in such barrels, but Californians were then using American white oak casks or redwood tanks.

Zellerbach died in 1964 before the full weight of his idea came to rest on his colleagues. But the wines he made stirred such interest that every California grower of varietals found himself obliged during the 1960s to decide for or against using European barrels in his cellars.

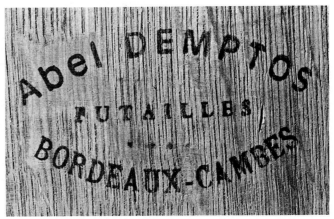

The last coopers

The art of making barrels—
coopering—has almost
disappeared from California. A
few firms linger, making slant
or straight-sided tanks from
milled redwood or oak. A few
others operate as restorers of
used barrels from other parts of
the United States or Europe. But
the need for people who know
how to hand cut and bend
staves from oak has nearly
disappeared with improved
transportation that favors doing
the work where the wood
grows, in Ohio or adjoining
states or in the commercial
forests of France, Germany and
Yugoslavia.
    One of the curiosities of
California is that none of its
several abundant varieties of
oak is among the best sorts for
making wine casks.

RESTORERS OF CASKS. Pamela and Kenneth
Marr restore worn oak barrels at their
Healdsburg ranch, one of several such family
firms in the North Coast counties.
No nail or glue holds a barrel together—
only a tight fit and hoops. Once a barrel begins
to leak, it must be disassembled, each stave
cleaned, then put back together again and
caulked tight. The staves are numbered in
sequence by the original maker to aid in the
process. Old inner tubes make handy jigs for
the reassembly phase.

TANK FACTORY. Bellagio is one of two firms in Healdsburg and one of several in the state specializing in the milling and assembly of large redwood or oak tanks for wineries.

IN TIMES GONE BY. At the turn of the century, when San Francisco was full of Italian and German coopering firms, the capacities of oak oval casks were scribed on the fronts with a compass-like tool. The symbols have passed out of memory. Somehow, this set of circles and slashes means 1,355 gallons. Almost every old oak oval of 500 to 2,000 gallons has one of these marks on its face, faint beneath the coats of varnish.

OL' SOL AND THE SOLERA. Sherry is made by exposing white wine to air and warmth. Sebastiani is one of few wineries in California to use direct heat from the sun. A Solera, indoors or out, is a vertical aging system. The newest wine is in the top row, the oldest in the bottom. Wine is bottled only from the bottom row, which is refilled from the row above, and so on to the top.

In the Valley of the Moon

ROOM FOR MORE. Sebastiani keeps its red wines in a steadily expanding cellar of small oak barrels.

At the turn of the century, as many as a hundred wineries operated within the small confines of the Valley of the Moon. During the 1940s, their number dwindled to fewer than 10. Of that small company, only the Samuele Sebastiani winery amounted to much as a business. Even the Sebastianis dealt mostly in bulk wines.

There still are fewer than 10 wineries in the Valley of the Moon, but the district is plainly on the upswing. A newspaperman named Frank Bartholomew revived Haraszthy's long-idle Buena Vista during World War II (and has since sold it to Young's Market Company of Los Angeles). J. D. Zellerbach founded Hanzell in the mid-1950s. The Sebastiani family began turning away from bulk wine and toward its own label in the late 1950s and early 1960s. A family named Lee bought the old Pagani Brothers winery in Kenwood, turning it in 1970 from a bulk winery into one devoted to varietals under the new Kenwood label. Other, smaller cellars have come into being in the past few years, including Z-D.

THE SEBASTIANIS. Samuele Sebastiani (above right) founded his first winery in Sonoma in 1895. His son August (above), has operated the family firm since Samuele's death in 1946. August's son Sam has begun to accept responsibilities in the management of the company.
In addition to being a winemaker, August Sebastiani is a widely recognized breeder of waterfowl, maintaining a large bird farm on one piece of property and a bird refuge on another. He is one of a surprising number of winemakers who excel at some second interest.

CHANGE OF SCENE. The Kenwood Vineyards in the town of the same name used to be a country jug winery serving a purely local trade. Owner Martin Lee used to be a San Francisco police detective.

After Lee and his family acquired the winery they shifted the focus of production from jug generics to fifth-bottles of varietals. However, for all the people who remember the place as the Pagani Brothers, the Lees continue to make and sell jug wines.

A PLACE FOR NEW IDEAS 🍇 123

Alexander, a new valley of vines

DAUGHTER & TROTTER. Russ Green's daughter tours the family vineyard in style.

Most of California's wine districts came into being because somebody familiar with winegrowing recognized signs remindful of some other place of vinous worth.

The Alexander Valley owes its blossoming as a vineyard district to one man's nostalgia for the Russian River swimming hole of his youth. Russell Green bought property on a big oxbow of the Russian River east of Healdsburg to regain a swimming hole. He planted grapes as an afterthought, and against local wisdom. When his vines prospered beyond all expectation, others came running. The grape acreage jumped from none in 1958 to 2,000 in 1972.

GROWTH STOCK. More vineyard acreage crops up each year in the Alexander Valley. Cooled by a loop of the Russian River that hides in the long row of trees, the region hovers between Region II and Region III according to the climate system devised by the University of California. In the upper photo, the young Cabernet Sauvignon vines in the foreground belong to an independent grower. In the photo at left, the newly planted vines belong to Sonoma Vineyards.

A PLACE FOR NEW IDEAS 🍇 125

MODERN TIMES. Sonoma Vineyards exemplifies contemporary functional design in wineries.

THE MEN WHO. Rod Strong launched Sonoma Vineyards. Russ Green revived Simi.

RESTORATION. Simi typifies pre-electric hillside architecture. Montepulciano was an old alias.

Revival in Healdsburg

Healdsburg sits at the hub of four valleys full of grapes: Alexander to the east, Dry Creek to the west, and the main course of the Russian River to the north and south. At the turn of the century, the town was the center of a fairly famous wine district. For a variety of reasons that fame died down. Local cellars went out of business, or applied themselves to the anonymous business of making bulk wine.

The new vineyards in the Alexander Valley seem to have rekindled old fires. Simi has been restored to its ancient prominence. New wineries called Dry Creek, Sonoma Vineyards and Souverain already are major names in town. Still more new cellars are in formative stages.

All of this activity has jostled several of the one-time bulk wineries into developing their own labels.

... Revival in Healdsburg

Several old-line, family-owned wineries around Healdsburg have survived since Prohibition by making generic table wines to be sold in bulk. Most of them now are developing labels of their own, and turning toward varietal wines. Zinfandel leads most of the lists, but there are Cabernet Sauvignons, Petite Sirahs and French Colombards as well. Pedroncelli, a few miles north of Healdsburg in Geyersville is one of the first and most prominent of the one-time bulk wineries to launch out in this direction. Foppiano is another. Cambiaso, with new owners, is yet a third.

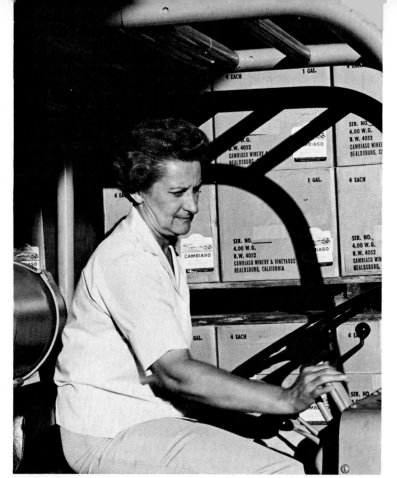

THE MANAGER. In a small winery, the boss does everything. At Cambiaso, G. M. Rita Ivy even drives forklift.

THE VETERAN. Frank Nervo has only recently retired from making varietal wine in bulk and sold his fine old stone cellar.

BUILT TO LAST. At the turn of the century, stone buildings such as Nervo's were typical of Sonoma wineries.

Echoes of an earlier era

At the north end of the Alexander Valley, the venerable Soda Rock winery sits right alongside State Route 128, as it has since the 1930s. Over on West Dry Creek Road, Chris Fredson sits out in plain view while the Frei Brothers winery secludes itself at the end of a long private lane. The Seghesio family has two wineries, one on a back street in Healdsburg, the other on a fine vineyard flanking US 101 near Asti. And so it goes.

No matter how visible the winery buildings might be to a traveler, the names remain unknown to wine drinkers. There is not one bottle of labeled wine to be had from any one of these cellars. Everything they make goes elsewhere in tank trucks or cars, to be bottled by Italian Swiss Colony, or The Christian Brothers, or Paul Masson, or—especially—E & J Gallo.

These are wines that never would acquire a label in Europe, where people habitually buy nameless wines from the barrel at a corner store. In this country, where all wine is formally bottled and branded, the odd corners of Sonoma and other counties must make their wines well enough to satisfy the man whose name eventually goes onto the bottle.

SOURCE FOR GALLO. The Sonoma Cooperative winery at Windsor sells all of its wine to the big firm of E & J Gallo in Modesto. It is one of several that does so.

HANDSOME BUT ANONYMOUS. The Seghesio winery near Asti is strikingly set against rolling Sonoma hills, but all of the wine made here goes to market under other labels.

NEWCOMER. Lumberman Bernard Fetzer built his winery in the Redwood Valley area in 1968.

Mendocino — gaining identity

THE OLD HANDS. John (left) and George Parducci are the second generation of their family to make wine in Ukiah. Their father founded the family business in 1932.

Wine grapes have been a part of the Mendocino County landscape around Ukiah for a good long time. In spite of that, the region has been largely anonymous for lack of home-grown wineries to build its reputation. Only one, Parducci, has been present as consistently as the grapes have. The Parduccis have at last acquired some substantial neighbors. One is Cresta Blanca, a part of the Guild Wineries and Distilleries. Another is Weibel, which has added a Mendocino winery to its original one in Alameda County.

Along with these large firms have come small cellars, such as Fetzer and Husch, whose owners are planting pioneer vineyards in Redwood Valley and the region around Boonville, 20 miles west of Ukiah.

Most of the wine is red.

CHOICES, CHOICES. Fred McCrea grows some of Napa's most famous grapes on his mountainous vineyard, called Stony Hill. Some of Stony Hill's closest challengers grow down on the valley floor, which gives hobbyists evidence for any position they wish to take in the argument about hill versus valley vineyards. The whole of the Napa Valley offers subtle choices to winemakers so the winemakers can offer subtle challenges to wine drinkers.

The Napa Valley looks old and settled and tranquil, the way wine country is supposed to look.

Long straight rows of vines carpet much of the long, straight valley floor, and curving rows blanket the steep hills where there is soil enough to hold roots. Imposing stone buildings full of fine oak casks complete the image of a place where wine is foremost.

It is not so much that Napa is uncommonly old among California wine districts. In fact, vines came to the valley a bit late. A settler named George Yount planted a vineyard for his own use in the 1840s. A German emigrant named Charles Krug made the first commercial wines in 1861, a long decade behind Sonoma and some 25 years behind Los Angeles.

The image arises more because vines and wines permeate more thoroughly in Napa than anywhere else in the state. All told, the vineyards came to 16,000 acres as of 1972. The most generous estimate is that the valley will hold no more than 25,000 acres if every scrap of arable land goes to the grape. Also, 39 wine cellars share the vineyards, a density averaging out at one cellar for each mile of State Route 29, the artery that splits the valley lengthwise from Carneros on the south to Calistoga on the north.

What sets the Napa Valley still further apart from the other districts is the obvious sense of continuity. Wine has changed very slowly in its 6,000 years of history. This valley retains the ancient tempos. Krug's old buildings still hold wine. So do a good many of the other nineteenth-century cellars. A great deal of ancient equipment lurks forgotten in sheds, or sits on display, polished for visitors to admire. But now and again somebody in one of the cellars does something useful with an outdated piece of gear because the thing works. Most important, the pioneer names are to be found not only on signposts and winery doors, but on mailboxes and payrolls.

4
The Napa Valley
Subtle choices

Who makes wine where

Within the narrow confines of the Napa Valley, the overwhelming emphasis is on varietal table wines. With the exception of the two specialists in Champagne—Hanns Kornell and Schramsberg—all of the valley wineries produce varietals. A few are small, estate-like cellars. Most of the familiar old names draw grapes from several vineyards spaced throughout the valley. A few have vineyards outside Napa.

Beaulieu Vineyard Rutherford 94573
Beringer 2000 Main Street, St. Helena 94574
Burgess Cellars PO Box 282, St. Helena 94574
Carneros Creek 1285 Dealy Lane, Napa 94558
Caymus Vineyards PO Box 268, Rutherford 94573
Chappellet Vineyard Pritchard Hill, St. Helena 94574
Chateau Montelena 1429 Tubbs Lane, Calistoga 94515
The Christian Brothers PO Box 420, Napa 94558
Clos du Val 5330 Silverado Trail, Napa 94558
Cuvaison 4560 Silverado Trail, Calistoga 94515
Diamond Creek 1500 Diamond Mountain Road, Calistoga 94515
Franciscan PO Box 407, Rutherford 94573
Freemark Abbey PO Box 410, St. Helena 94574
Heitz Cellars 500 Taplin Road, St. Helena 94574
Inglenook c/o United Vintners, 601 Fourth Street, San Francisco 94107
Hanns Kornell PO Box 249, St. Helena 94574
Charles Krug PO Box 191, St. Helena 94574
Louis M. Martini PO Box 112, St. Helena 94574
Mayacamas 1155 Lokoya Road, Napa 94558
Robert Mondavi PO Box 106, Oakville 94562
Mount Veeder 1999 Mt. Veeder Road, Napa 94558
Nichelini 2349 Lower Chiles Road, St. Helena 94574
Oakville PO Box 394, Oakville 94562
Joseph Phelps 200 Taplin Road, St. Helena 94574
Pope Valley 6613 Pope Valley Road, St. Helena 94574
Schramsberg Calistoga 94515
Spring Mountain 2805 Spring Mountain Road, St. Helena 94574
Stag's Leap Wine Cellars 5766 Silverado Trail, Napa 94558
Sterling Vineyards 1111 Dunaweal Lane, Calistoga 94515
Stonegate 1183 Dunaweal Lane, Calistoga 94515
Stony Hill PO Box 308, St. Helena 94574
Sutter Home 277 St. Helena Highway South, St. Helena 94574
Villa Mt. Eden PO Box 147, Oakville 94562
Yverdon 3728 Spring Mountain Road, St. Helena 94574

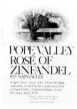

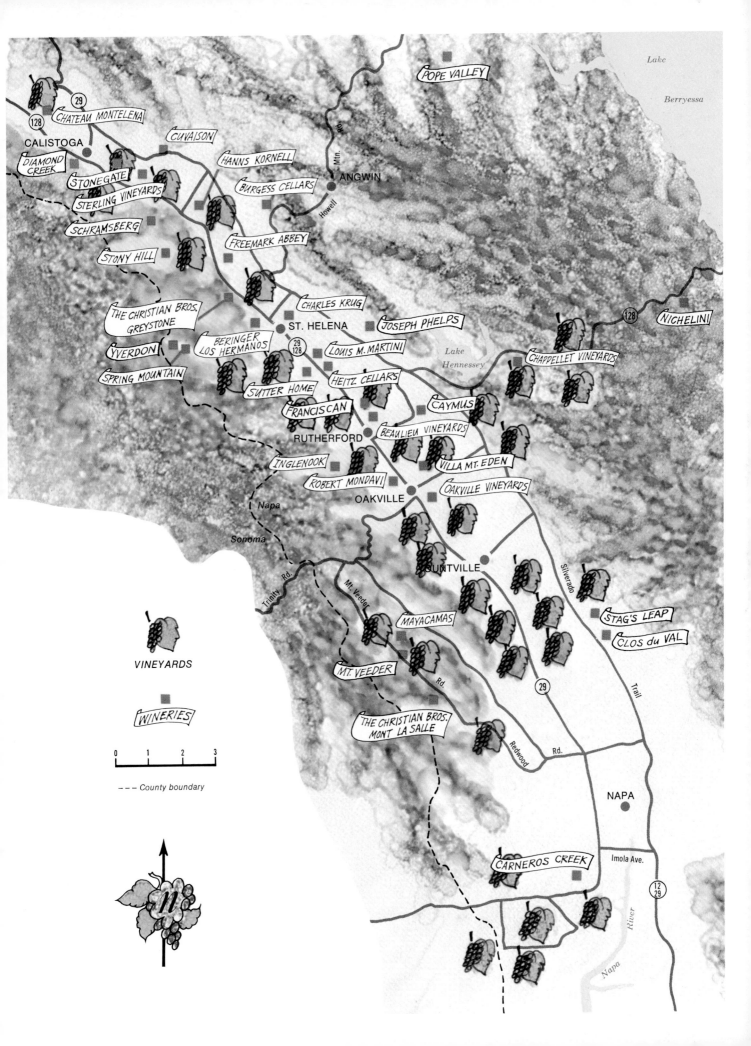

POPE VALLEY

Lake

Berryessa

CHATEAU MONTELENA

CALISTOGA

CUVAISON

DIAMOND CREEK

STONEGATE

HANNS KORNELL

ANGWIN

STERLING VINEYARDS

BURGESS CELLARS

SCHRAMSBERG

FREEMARK ABBEY

STONY HILL

CHARLES KRUG

NICHELINI

THE CHRISTIAN BROS. GREYSTONE

ST. HELENA

JOSEPH PHELPS

CHAPPELLET VINEYARDS

BERINGER LOS HERMANOS

YVERDON

LOUIS M. MARTINI

Lake Hennessey

SPRING MOUNTAIN

HEITZ CELLARS

SUTTER HOME

CAYMUS

FRANCISCAN

BEAULIEU VINEYARDS

RUTHERFORD

VILLA MT. EDEN

INGLENOOK

OAKVILLE VINEYARDS

ROBERT MONDAVI

OAKVILLE

Napa

Sonoma

Silverado

YOUNTVILLE

STAG'S LEAP

CLOS du VAL

MAYACAMAS

MT. VEEDER

VINEYARDS

THE CHRISTIAN BROS. MONT LA SALLE

WINERIES

0   1   2   3

Redwood   Rd.

NAPA

--- County boundary

Imola Ave.

CARNEROS CREEK

River

Napa

IT LOOKS THE SAME, BUT. Veteran
winemakers in the valley swear
they can identify a dusty
taste imparted to wine by these
soils around Rutherford town.
There is a geologic difference from
other Napa soils.

SURVIVORS OF THE PAST. Charles
Krug built his winery estate (upper
right) in 1871. Inglenook (lower right)
was built by Gustav Nybom in 1887.
Both are active wineries today. The old
Debret et Priet estate (below), built
in 1886, is now the private residence
of vineyardist Rene di Rosa.

MONUMENT OF MONUMENTS. Greystone Cellars, now owned by The Christian Brothers, was completed in 1889. William Bowers Bourn set out to own the largest stone winery in the world, and did. A man of enormous wealth, Bourn spent $2 million to realize his ambition.

The Napa Valley's long legacy

The current wine boom is not the first one the Napa Valley has enjoyed. During the 1880s and 1890s there was a tremendous burst of interest in wines from the region, setting off a subsidiary boom of monumental winery architecture.

In the most concrete of fashions, fine buildings bespeak serious purpose among winemakers of the region. The fact that the most striking of them were rehabilitated for winemaking as soon as Prohibition ended bears witness to their power as symbols of hope. Their endurance through the lean years before 1963 says still more about the people who keep them full of wine.

The monumentalist's monument is Greystone Cellars. Beringer, Inglenook, and Charles Krug are nearly as striking. In addition to these structures in plain view, others of equal style seclude themselves in folded hills above the valley floor. Some of these hidden gems have begun to be wineries again, too.

The heroic builders of yore

At the beginning, the Napa Valley drew its winery owners and winemakers from every corner of Europe. Gustav Nybom, builder of Inglenook, was a Finn and a retired sea captain. William Bowers Bourn, who launched Greystone, and H. W. Crabb, who owned ToKalon, were Anglo types. The French were represented by a whole series of partnerships, including Debret & Priet and Brun & Chaix. But the era 1870-1900 had a predominantly German flavor, one built on solid enough foundations to contribute most of the pioneer names and buildings still enduring today. Charles Krug started commercial winemaking in the valley in 1861 after a short apprenticeship with Agoston Haraszthy in Sonoma. On Krug's heels came the brothers Jacob and Frederick Beringer and Jacob Schram. Now-faded names like J. Thomann, C. J. Beerstecher, and G. Groezinger were major figures in their time.

FAMILY PORTRAIT. Jacob Beringer (fourth from left) and Frederick Beringer (sixth from left) pose with cellarmen in front of the caves they had excavated in 1877. The small boy, C. T. Beringer, ran the family firm after Prohibition. In 1970 the fourth generation of Beringers sold the old family property to Nestle, the Swiss food corporation.

GUSTAV NYBOM   CHARLES KRUG

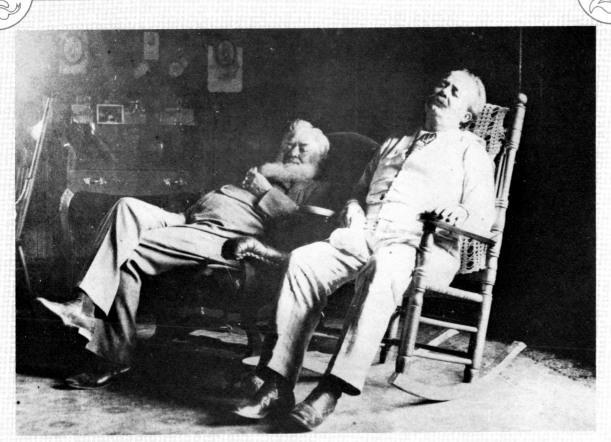

FRIENDLY COMPETITORS. Jacob Schram (left) and Charles Carpy relax in Schram's parlor, looking as though they had just worked a very good deal. Schram's family no longer makes wine, although his old property is again active as Schramsberg Champagne Cellars. Carpy's winery is gone, but a descendant is a principal in Freemark Abbey.

GEORGES DE LATOUR. He founded Beaulieu Vineyard at the turn of the century and ran it until his death in 1940. His wife and daughter continued BV until 1969, when they sold the winery and most of its vineyards to Heublein.

JOHN DANIEL. The great nephew of Gustav Nybom retained Inglenook as a classic estate until 1964, when he sold to United Vintners, which in turn was bought by Heublein. Inglenook and BV adjoin each other in Rutherford.

The rebuilders

Directly after Prohibition, some 60 optimists started wineries in the Napa Valley. However, the Great Depression and World War II produced conditions only slightly more attractive to winemakers than Prohibition had. In the long struggle against poor odds, it was a small core of stubborn people who restored the valley to the vinous eminence it had held before 1919.

Three pre-Prohibition wine families—the Beringers, the deLatours at Beaulieu, and John Daniel (as Nybom's inheritor) at Inglenook—survived the lapse and were able to take up where they had left off. Of the first wave of newcomers, only The Christian Brothers, the Louis Martinis (father and son), and the Mondavi family (as new owners of Charles Krug's old winery) proved durable. Later, in the 1940s, came the first small stylists, such as Lee Stewart of Souverain and Fred McCrea of Stony Hill.

FATHER AND SON. Louis P. Martini (left) operates the family winery founded in 1934 by his late father, Louis M. Martini (above). Louis P. learned at his father's elbow and at the University of California at Davis. Louis M. was the unofficial dean of California winemakers for many years before his death, at 84, in 1974. He also was a legendary chef.

THE LIBRARY. The family Mondavi has hidden away in a back corner of the Charles Krug winery a library of Krug wines reaching back to 1940, the year Cesare Mondavi bought the property. After his death in 1959, his widow, Rosa (right) ran the winery, with son Peter (left). Since Rosa's death in 1976, Peter has carried on the family business.

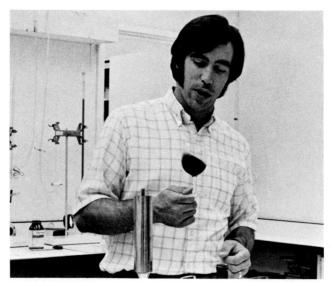

FATHERS AND SONS. Michael Mondavi manages the winery for his father, Robert Mondavi. The Mondavi family goes back one more generation in the valley. Cesare Mondavi settled in 1935.

The heroic builders of now

One measure of the extent of the new wine boom is the current flurry of architecturally distinctive winery construction. Some buildings were built by old valley families, the case with Robert Mondavi. Some have been built by men who put in long apprenticeships with other wineries, as Joe Heitz of Heitz Cellars did. Many—Chappellet, Souverain and Sterling included—are the products of newcomers to the valley and to wine.

THE PYRAMID. The Chappellet winery snugs into its site high above Lake Hennessey. Within, form follows function. Tall tanks cluster at the center. Small barrels rim the edges.

BOW TO THE PAST. The Robert Mondavi winery pays architectural tribute to California's missions. Built in 1966, it was the first major winery erected in the valley since 1935.

APPRENTICE. Donn Chappellet has a diligent picker in 4-year-old son Dominic. He may follow in his father's footsteps, but mother is his coach.

147

CRUSADER'S HABITAT. Sterling Vineyards' new winery was patterned after chapels built in the Greek Isles by Christian crusaders of medieval times. The building was completed in 1973. Its owners are the proprietors of an international trading company based in San Francisco.

WITH A BOW TO OLD NAPA. The traditional Napa Valley hay barn served as the architectural model for this cellar, originally built as Souverain, but re-named Oak Knoll Cellars by new owners in 1976.

RENAISSANCE. The old vineyards of Chateau Chevalier have been replanted by James Frew, and the winery has been returned by Gregg Bissonette to a life it first knew in 1891.

New faces in old places

In the early years of Napa winemaking, hillside vineyards were the most economical kind because planting vines on slopes was the only means of avoiding undue frost damage. Now, hillsides are less economical than the frost-guarded valley floor because they are remote from transportation and ill-adapted to mechanical farming. As a result, the dozens of old hill wineries have been slow to return to life in the long recovery from Prohibition.

Lee Stewart at the original Souverain and Jack Taylor at Mayacamas were two of the first, in the 1940s. With the boom in wine, more and more of the old stone buildings have been restored to vinous life.

UP TOP. Mayacamas Vineyards has its wine cellars underground, but at a high elevation in the volcanic hills separating Napa and Sonoma Counties. Proprietor Bob Travers tastes a Cabernet Sauvignon in the old cave, dug out by a man named Fisher in 1889. Travers has owned Mayacamas since 1967.

ANDRE TCHELISTCHEFF. Pick late to make a red.

VERSATILE. Pinot noir grapes made both wines.

JACK DAVIES. Pick early to make a white Champagne.

Possibilities
with
Pinot noir

For Jack Davies, perfect Pinot noir grapes are picked at 18 to 19 degrees Balling (a measure of sugar) and 1.1 acid. For Andre Tchelistcheff, the same grape is at its peak when the sugar measures 23 to 24 Balling and the acid balances at .9.

Davies, the proprietor of Schramsberg, uses Pinot noir for a sparkling white wine in the classic style of Champagne. He picks his grapes as early in the season as possible to minimize color. Later steps in the *methode champenoise* compensate for the low alcohol level from low sugar.

Tchelistcheff in his long career at Beaulieu used the variety to make red wine after the fashion of Burgundy. He could wait far into the season for sugar to build and color to intensify in the grapes so his wine would be rich and dark.

The two men—friends—represent opposite ends of the spectrum of opinion about Napa Pinot noir. Variations in wines from the close-knit community of Napa winemakers are a fascination to wine hobbyists.

OTHER MEN, OTHER IDEAS, Brother Timothy (at left) is the cellarmaster of The Christian Brothers. Like Beaulieu, his winery makes Pinot Noir as a red. Unlike Beaulieu, the Brothers do not vintage-date their wine, preferring instead to blend lots from two or more vintages to achieve their standard of taste. On other points of blending and aging, Tchelistcheff and Brother Timothy sometimes agree, sometimes do not. For hobbyists, the game is to sort out resulting distinctions of flavor, preferably in blind tastings.

Hanns Kornell (below) is, with Davies, a Champagne specialist in the valley. In this case, both men hold very similar views on blending, aging, and the other techniques of Champagne-making. They differ on grape varieties. Kornell prefers Riesling as the base grape in his wines rather than the French varieties—Pinot noir and Chardonnay—favored by Davies. Again, hobbyists have a fascinating riddle to solve in blind tastings.

Pick, pick, pick

CAGEY VETERANS. Wise pickers sprint in the cool of dawn, then ease off in the heat of the day.

FILLERUP.

DEFOLIATED. Winemakers love no leaf.

Pickers have a different set of standards for grapes
from those of either winemakers or wine drinkers. The
question is not taste but how fruit comes off the
vines. Pickers hate Chenin blanc from old vineyards
because the grape clusters grow on tough stems
way down inside an impenetrable thicket of canes.
Cabernet Sauvignon, on the other hand, is a
choice assignment because the variety bears a fairly
heavy crop of grapes that stand out, ready
to be plucked.

In any variety, the game is to pick each cluster of
healthy fruit but hardly any leaves at all and for each
man to work at a sustained rate of 2,000 pounds per day.

COOL, CLEAR WATER. Harvest work is lamentably warm and dusty.

TRANQUIL TO SEE. A small crew works to fill a big gondola at a vineyard near Rutherford.

From vine to winery

PARADE ON MAIN. During the harvest, St. Helena even smells vinous.

END OF THE ROAD. At Heitz Cellars.

With vineyards scattered for miles to take advantage of micro-climates, wineries have adopted the gondola as a prime mode of moving grapes from field to crusher. Gondolas, not built for speed on the highway, cause slow-going for harvest season traffic in the valley. In spite of that, they have speeded up the work of turning grapes into wine. The old method of loading lug boxes onto trucks one at a time and unloading them the same way was not quick.

THE ONE AND ONLY. At the Nichelini winery in the hills east of the Napa Valley there is one workable Roman press, a contrivance that came to full flower in Medieval times. The next nearest one is in a wine museum in Beaune, France. Jim Nichelini used his until the early 1960s, and keeps it as a souvenir of vintages that pressed out very slowly.

Presses, old and new

Romantic though the ancient basket press is, it has two outstanding flaws in the eyes of winemakers: it is an imprecise machine, and it is a slow and laborious contraption to use.

The search for a better press has been a continuing part of the technological revolution in winemaking. Some improvements are mechanical variations on the old basket. Others revolutionize the principles of pressing.

Basket press

A metal sole plate winds down on a threaded center column, exerting pressure through a set of wood blocks and a solid wood disc the same diameter as the basket.

The grapes are squeezed under slowly mounting pressure within a coarse filter (usually burlap) that holds skins and seeds while the juice trickles out between staves of the basket. As it collects in a pan, the juice is either dumped or pumped into a fermenting tank.

The hand-operated basket press has to be dismantled after each charge, emptied by hand, and reloaded the same way.

Horizontal basket

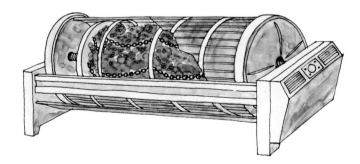

Presses of the Vaslin or Howard type have motor-driven end walls that press inward within the basket on a threaded column. The walls can be retracted once a carefully gauged pressure is reached. Then, a motor revolves the whole basket at high speed. Chains strung lengthwise within the basket loosen the pressed cake. The loosened cake means that far less pressure is required for the second pressing.

Juice flows between closely set wood staves or through fine-mesh stainless steel screen. A pan collects it.

These presses are emptied by rotating the basket upside down after the gates have been opened.

Air-pressure press

Air-pressure presses, pioneered by the German firm of Willmes, reverse the principle of pressing from the basket types. They squeeze from the inside out.

The press is a horizontal cylinder with an inflatable neoprene tube suspended lengthwise inside. This tube exerts a very slight pressure outward, squeezing a thin layer of grapes between itself and the fine-mesh stainless steel skin of the cylinder.

As in the case of horizontal baskets, the cylinder can be rotated (with a deflated tube) to loosen the cake. (In all presses, the ideal is several gentle pressings, rather than one severe one.)

These presses empty in the same way as the Vaslin or Howard types.

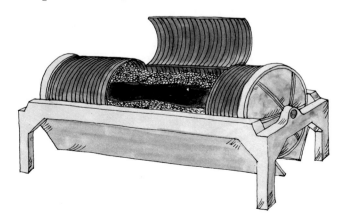

157

The makings of a vintage year

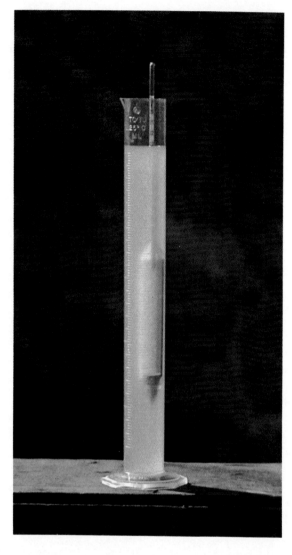

Degrees Balling	Specific Gravity	Potential Alcohol
26	1.108	15.5
25	1.104	14.9
24	1.099	14.1
23	1.094	13.4
22	1.090	12.6
21	1.085	11.9
20	1.081	11.2
19	1.076	10.5
18	1.072	9.8

BIRTH OF A JOHANNISBERG. Freshly crushed must of the 1972 Johannisberg Riesling at Freemark Abbey registers 23° Balling on the saccharometer, an ideal sugar level for the variety. The conversion scale of degrees Balling to percent alcohol is only rough; the actual alcohol can vary slightly depending on the yeast strain used to ferment and on the fermentation temperature. Also, the winemaker can stop the fermentation while some sugar remains if he wants the wine to be faintly sweet. Cold stops the action.

Winemakers look for grapes with certain balances of sugar and acid when they have hopes for a year of outstanding wines. In the Napa Valley, an ideal balance for dry wines would be 22.5° Balling of sugar, with .85 to .9 per cent of tartaric acid in the must. ("Must" is the name for grape juice on the way to becoming wine.) Sugar ($C_6H_{12}O_6$) yields alcohol (C_2H_5OH) along with carbon dioxide (CO_2). Alcohol and acid together are the carriers of flavor and the sources of stable good health in a wine.

The unbalancing truth of the matter, though, is that perfect musts can yield ordinary wine while less promising ones turn into superb wine.

The way a wine is fermented establishes its basic character.

All white wine is fermented in closed tanks, without skins or seeds in contact with the juice. Those intended to be light and fresh ferment very slowly at refrigerated temperatures in the low 50s or high 40s. White wines meant to endure for years ferment faster at warmer temperatures—into the mid 60s. Chardonnay is the prime example.

Red wines ferment in open tanks with the skins and seeds in contact with the juice and at temperatures ranging from the low 70s through the high 80s. Light wines stay on the skins for only a few days, just long enough to acquire color. The musts of wines intended to age for a decade and more may be kept on the skins for a week, even two, to extract all the color and as much other stuffing as possible.

PUMPING OVER. The color in red wines comes from the skins rather than the juice. To extract maximum color, the winemaker at Beaulieu pumps wine from the bottom of the tank over the solid cap of Pinot noir skins and seeds that floats atop the seething must.

TIME BUYERS. In addition to their intended role as fermenting tanks, these stainless steel vessels at Sterling Vineyards are sometimes used to hold new red wines in a state of suspended animation until they can be moved into small oak barrels for final aging.

What to keep wine in to keep it happy

REDWOOD OR WHITE? Heitz Cellars can choose between oak tanks (on the left) and redwood.

Wine in its diversity demands all kinds of aging vessels to help preserve the differences. The essence of the winemaker's choice is how much flavor he wishes to overlay as a complication to the natural flavors of the grapes. Fresh, springy whites and rosés want almost nothing added. Age-worthy reds can profit from a subtle bouquet of oak.

Stainless steel and glass-lined steel tanks are neutral. Large redwood tanks are nearly so. Oak imparts more flavor than other woods. The smaller the barrel, the more pronounced its effect on the wine.

A winemaker develops the style of his wine by using one kind of cooperage alone or several in combination. Time is the other variable at his disposal.

REDWOOD FOREST. These tanks at Louis M. Martini hold 30,000 gallons apiece. They are valuable for any wine, great or small, that the winemaker wants to mature slowly.

The bigger the wine
the smaller the barrel

Although there are exceptions—with wine
there always are exceptions—most
winemakers use their smallest barrels to age
their biggest wines, the varietals of
forceful character.

Mountain Red tends to go directly
from a large redwood tank to bottle, but
small barrels hold most of the Napa
Valley's Chardonnays, Pinot Noirs, and
Cabernet Sauvignons for some part of their
two to three-year aging cycle. Small
barrels hasten the maturity of these wines
by offering more surface for them to
act against.

OAK OVALS. Handsome but hard to maintain, casks are
giving way to straight-sided oak tanks.

THE FINISHING TOUCH. Different kinds of oak impart different flavors. Charles Krug has this gallery
of American oak and another cellar full of European oak barrels.

Learning at a liquid library

Having developed subtle differences among their wines, the Napa Valley's winemakers have felt obliged to offer their clientele practical instruction in advanced wine appreciation. In addition to maintaining traditional tasting rooms for visitors, the winemakers support four to eight weekend wine courses each year. The courses are operated by the Napa Valley Wine Library Association, which draws its faculties from the roster of winemakers.

From Friday afternoon through Sunday, students taste wines doctored to demonstrate faults, then move on to comparative tastings of unlabelled wines drawn from the wineries' own stocks.

Privileged tours of wineries and informal lectures amplify the experience.

FINE POINTS. A master winemaker explains how and why wines are filtered.

THE SCHOOLHOUSE. At recess, students talk over lectures and tastings.

TAKING IT FROM THE TOP. A professional vineyardist demonstrates why good vineyards yield good wines.

THE REASON FOR IT ALL. At tasting sessions, course members taste several examples of each major varietal, score them, then compare their reactions with those of a winemaster.

GUESS. The staff will not say who made a wine, no matter how good it is.

READY. Running vine rows straight is a major surveying job.

Expanding the supply

With the growing awareness of wine in the United States, vineyard acreage in the Napa Valley expanded from 10,000 in 1959 to 16,300 in 1972.

For a landowner, developing new vineyard means spending something like $1,700 per acre over three years before any returns come in. The trick, obviously, is to plant varieties that will fetch good prices, which means correctly guessing which wines people will be drinking five years into the future.

SET. New vineyards hold about 575 plants per acre. The mature yield: about five tons.

STAKE DRIVER. Machines do the work in flat vineyards but not in hilly ones.

BUNNY FOIL. Rabbits love a salad of juicy young grape leaves.

GROW. Tender young vines reach no more than halfway up their stakes in the first growing season.

Fine graftsmanship

Ever since a tiny root louse called phylloxera *vastatrix* made its ruinous appearance in European and Californian coastal vineyards in the mid-1880s, growers in affected regions have been forced to graft fruitwood of the tender *Vitis vinifera* onto rootstock from hardy American native vines. As always in winey matters, there are at least two schools of thought. In this case, the traditional method is field budding and the newer idea of bench grafts.

In field budding, the rootstock is planted in new vineyards and allowed to grow for a season, then a tiny chip bud of Chardonnay or whatever is grafted onto the main stalk of the rootstock plant near ground level. If the bud takes, the top of the rootstock is lopped off the following spring, and the fruiting variety grows in its place. If the first bud does not take, a second try follows.

In bench grafting, a short length of fruitwood is fitted to a longer piece of rootstock somewhat in the way of tongue-in-groove wood, then the plant is potted and left to root. Once rooted, it goes into the vineyard.

In either case, the key is to get a perfect match between the cambium layers of fruitwood and rootstock so sap can flow between the two.

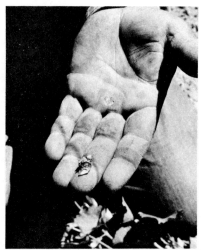

FIELD BUDDING. A delicate knife stroke cuts one bud from a cane of **Vitis vinifera**. This bud is then nestled into a matching cut on the rootstock, usually after a lubricating pass across the tongue of the vineyard worker. The bud is held in place with a length of rubber band.

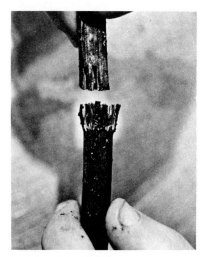

BENCH GRAFTING. After being matched in diameter and notched, lengths of rootstock and fruiting variety are joined end to end. Wax seals the graft. The plant is then rooted.

WATER OF LIFE. Dry California summers demand irrigation of new vineyards. Overhead mist is the coast counties choice because it also is an effective method of frost protection.

NATURE'S LITTLE HELPER.

NEW DAY DAWNING. The traditional view of a winery centers upon cobwebby cellars. That image has faded in the San Joaquin Valley. At a new winery like the E & J Gallo installation at Livingston, each tank is a controlled environment within itself. The roof is gone, along with the cellar. Exceptions do linger, a handful of hand-operated family wineries scattered throughout the valley.

In its sheer physical vastness, the San Joaquin Valley brooks no rival among California's wine districts. Its vineyards stretch 280 miles from Lodi in the north to Bakersfield in the south, with principal concentrations of vines at Lodi, Madera, Fresno, and Delano. The annual crush of grapes for wine runs upwards of 1.5 million tons—compared with 150,000 tons for all the coast counties put together.

The size of the valley seems to have inspired its winemakers to match their efforts to its scope. Just four companies market the great proportion of wines resulting from the awesome tonnage of grapes. The leader, far and away, is E. & J. Gallo, followed by United Vintners, the several divisions of Guild Wineries and Distilleries, and Franzia. Each uses grapes from the whole of the valley rather than any one part. This had had the effect of fusing the big valley into one district.

In essence the hot summers of the San Joaquin region make it a natural district for the production of Ports, Sherries, and other dessert wines. Indeed, the best of these wines made in California come from valley-grown grapes. But scientific vineyard management and winemaking techniques have allowed the emphasis of production to shift from dessert to table wines in recent years.

The San Joaquin Valley has vinous history. A man named George Krause had a sizable winery called Red Mountain in Stanislaus County by 1866. A Lee Eisen planted the first grapes at Fresno as early as 1873. Yet, compared to other parts of California, the vinous past has dimmed into insignificance in these vast reaches. The old names of pre-Prohibition winemaking have very nearly disappeared from memory, let alone use.

Somehow it is fitting. The outlook is entirely forward. Except for the work of a tiny handful of specialists, wine from the San Joaquin Valley reaches its highest peak in wineries that are as modern as they look.

5
San Joaquin Valley
Vineyard of the giants

Who makes wine where

The San Joaquin Valley is the source of a great proportion of California's inexpensive generic table wines, very nearly all of its Ports and Sherries, and all of its flavored Pop wines. Keeping track of labels is difficult because many firms use two or more names for their wines, while others do most of their business in bulk to other bottlers in and outside the state, selling only small amounts as a sideline. These labels represent a cross-section of wineries, but show only the principal brands of several firms.

Lodi

Barengo Cellars PO Box A, Acampo 95220
Coloma Cellars/Alexander 22291 N. De Vries Road, Lodi 94241
East-Side (Royal Host) 6100 E. Highway 12, Lodi 95240
Guild PO Box 519, Lodi 95240

Modesto-Escalon

Bella Napoli 21128 S. Austin Road, Manteca 95336
Bronco 6342 Bystrum Road, Ceres 95307
Cadlolo 1124 California Street, Escalon 95320
Delicato 12001 S. Highway 99, Manteca 95336
Franzia PO Box 697, Ripon 95366
E & J Gallo PO Box 1130, Modesto 95353

Fresno-Madera

Almaden (see page 66)
Growers PO Box 38, Cutler 93615
The Christian Brothers (see page 136)
Del Rey 5427 E. Central Avenue, Fresno 93725
Farnesi 2426 Almond Avenue, Sanger 93657
Ficklin 30246 Avenue 7½, Madera 93637
Gibson 1720 Academy Avenue, Sanger 93657
Landis 2068 E. Clayton Avenue, Fresno 93705
Paul Masson (see page 66)
Nonini 2640 N. Dickenson Avenue, Fresno 93705
Angelo Papagni 31754 Avenue 9, Madera 93637
Roma 3223 E. Church Avenue, Fresno 93714
United Vintners 601 Fourth Street, San Francisco 94107

Bakersfield

Bear Mountain (M. LaMont) PO Box 566, Lamont 93241
Giumarra Vineyards PO Bin 1969, Edison 93303
A. Perelli-Minetti & Sons (Ambassador) PO Box 818, Delano 93215

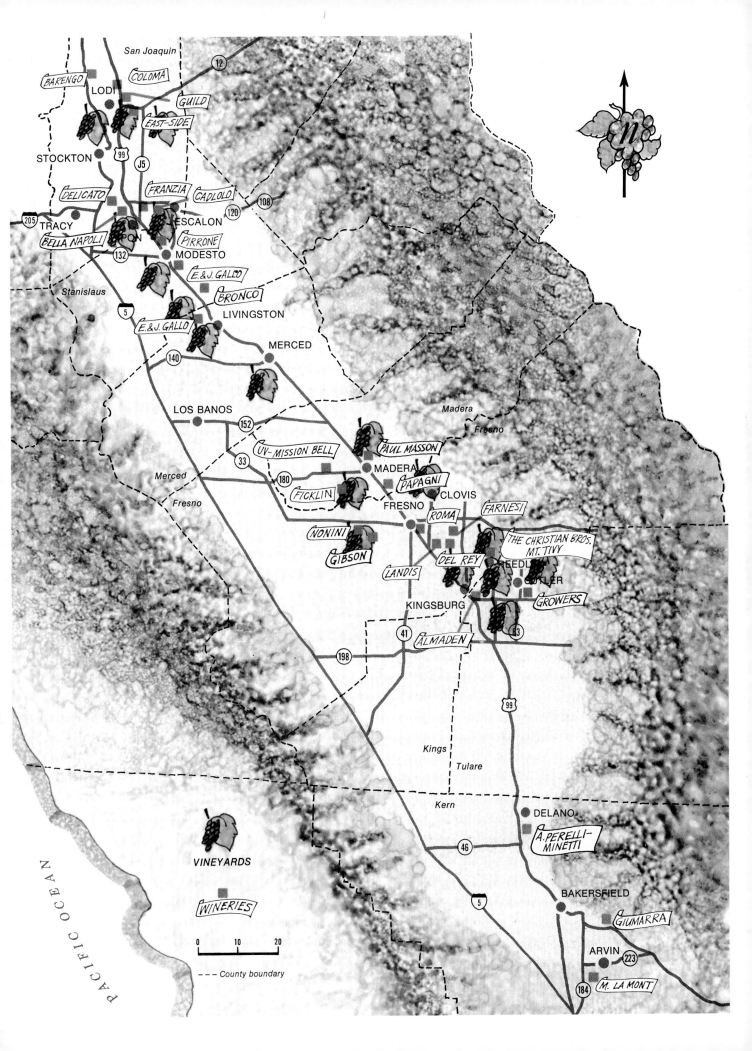

San Joaquin

BARENGO
LODI
COLOMA
GUILD
EAST-SIDE

STOCKTON
99
J5

DELICATO
FRANZIA
CADLOLO
108
120

TRACY
205
BELLA NAPOLI
RIPON
ESCALON
PIRRONE
MODESTO
132

Stanislaus

E.&J. GALLO
BRONCO

E.&J. GALLO
LIVINGSTON
5

140
MERCED

LOS BANOS
152

Madera
Fresno

UV-MISSION BELL
33
180
PAUL MASSON

Merced
FICKLIN
MADERA
PAPAGNI
CLOVIS

Fresno
FRESNO
FARNESI
ROMA

NONINI
THE CHRISTIAN BROS.
MT. TIVY

GIBSON
DEL REY
REEDLEY
CUTLER

LANDIS
GROWERS
KINGSBURG
63

41
ALMADEN

198
99

Kings
Tulare

Kern

DELANO
A. PERELLI-
MINETTI

VINEYARDS
46

WINERIES
5
BAKERSFIELD

GIUMARRA

0   10   20
ARVIN
223

- - - County boundary
184
M. LA MONT

PACIFIC OCEAN

N

THREE-WAY COUNTRY. The Central Valley has exaggerated size as a winegrowing district owing to the fact that it also supports table and raisin grapes among its vineyards. But it is big.

VINEYARD OF THE GIANTS 🍇 175

ONE OF THREE. E & J Gallo, faced with the geographic scope of the San Joaquin Valley, maintains this winery at Livingston and a similar one at Fresno as fermenting and storage facilities. The final aging and bottling of Gallo wines is done at the home winery in Modesto. Such use of multiple installations is typical of large wineries in California.

In the valley, big is BIG

In the 1972-73 directory of the North American wine industry published by *Wines & Vines*, the storage capacity of E & J Gallo is listed at 165,000,000 gallons, with another 50,000,000 gallons of fermentors.

United Vintners-Heublein follows along with 95,000,000 gallons. Guild has 50,788,000. Even a relative unknown like Bear Mountain has a capacity of 26,000,000.

In these wineries, science reaches its fullest flower in the wine industry. The quintessential goal is a product of unvarying characteristics. The volume of grapes—drawn from all over the state—allows compensation for vagaries of weather. Then, from crusher to bottle, the whole environment in which wine matures is maintained at rigorously defined standards. Sources of uncontrollable flavors are not even permitted on the premises, which explains the wholesale disappearance of wooden cooperage from large wineries in favor of stainless or glass-lined steel tanks.

E & J Gallo has emerged as the undisputed leader in California wine sales in part because of extraordinary marketing skills, but fully as much for being the most successful employer of quality control in its winemaking. The amazing fact is that the firm remains a family affair. Ernest and Julio Gallo started it with 100,000 gallons of wooden tanks in 1933. They and their families own it all in 1973.

JOHN B. CELLA

The forerunner

If there is any one man who turned the San Joaquin Valley away from a multitude of small wineries and toward a few big ones, it was John B. Cella with his Roma Winery in Fresno.

At the end of Prohibition, all of California's wine districts were in chaos, but none so much as the Big Valley. It never had been a bastion of family wine estates to the degree that the coast counties had been; the interruption of fourteen years from 1919 to 1933 had virtually stripped it of its experienced winemakers.

In essence, 1933 gave Cella a fair-sized vacuum to work in. Although there were powerful interests involved, nobody else had the same concentration of money, position, and the will to establish one label as a giant in the market. For years Cella built on a good start. When World War II came along and the country's distillers needed new products to replace the distilled spirits that had been conscripted by the government for defense use, Cella was able to sell the largest winery in the country to Schenley Industries.

Roma endured ups and downs thereafter. In 1972 Schenley sold the premises to the Guild Wineries and Distilleries, which operates Roma as a relatively small part of its total activities.

The physical plant has not been changed radically from the early 1940s, when it was the largest and most modern winery in California. The old brick buildings with their cargoes of casks and vats offer a nostalgic counterpoint to what is now, a mere thirty years later, large and modern.

GET 'EM WHILE THEY'RE HOT. In an infernal atmosphere of smoke, flame, and ear-shattering noise, champagne bottles come glowing out of their molds at the Madera Glass plant.

Do-it-yourself bottlemaking

Running one of the genuinely large wineries in the San Joaquin Valley is, among other things, an exercise in big-league logistics. It requires an orderly, cost-saving annual program for making and storing millions of gallons of wine, and moving millions of bottles and cartons into the winery empty and back out into the world full. One of the ways major producers keep close control over their operations is to do everything they can for themselves. The most dramatic examples of the trend are glass manufacturing plants operated by E & J Gallo at Modesto, and United Vintners at Madera.

TA POCKETA POCKETA. Although they look like something out of a Walter Mitty fantasy, big bottling lines in valley wineries run at the rate of 7,200 to 8,400 bottles an hour. They do an amazing amount of automated work, ridding bottles of oxygen so it cannot spoil the wine, filling them within a half-ounce tolerance, closing the tops with caps, applying and crimping the capsules that cover the necks, and, finally, coating labels with glue and sticking them in place. This line is at Guild.

OUTDOOR WINEMAKING. Increasingly, San Joaquin Valley wineries leave their aging tanks outdoors, without a vestige of building to protect them. Two factors allow this practice with no harm to the wines inside. First, the tanks run from 200,000 up to 600,000 gallons capacity each. A mass of liquid that large does not change temperature rapidly. In any case, each tank has a jacket linked to a heating and/or cooling system that can be used to regulate the internal temperatures within a degree. These tanks are part of United Vinters' Mission Bell winery at Madera.

Suddenly, Champagne

In 1907 a Frenchman named Eugene Charmat invented a means of getting bubbles into wine with far less trouble and expense than the ancient methods for making Champagne. Widely used around the world, the Charmat is almost the exclusive method for making modestly priced sparkling wines in the San Joaquin Valley.

In essence, Charmat sparkling wines—also known as bulk process—are made in tanks holding several hundred to several thousand gallons of wine rather than in individual bottles. (See page 112 for a description of the bottle fermented process.) In either case, a still wine is inoculated with yeast and a sweet grape syrup to set off a slight secondary fermentation. Charmat wines ferment quickly in their tanks. Soon after the fermentation has run its course, the now-sparkling wine is filtered and bottled under pressure. The process saves literally hundreds of steps compared to bottle fermented champagnes, in addition to years of time.

CHAMPAGNE BOTTLE. At Guild, 5,000-gallon glass-lined tanks hold the Charmat Champagnes during secondary fermentation and aging.

Going to run all night

To get San Joaquin Valley grapes at their optimum, the huge crop
must be picked as quickly as the small ones in the coast counties.
Size, coupled with unrelentingly flat terrain, makes the Big Valley a
more practical environment for mechanical harvesters than
for human pickers.

Running at a moderate pace, the machines can pick 12 tons an hour.
Pushed to the limit, they may harvest 24 tons per hour from a prolific
vineyard. They can—and do—pick at such rates around the clock.
The night operator needs only two headlights to steer by. Work halts
only at six-hour intervals, when the machines must be stopped
for 30 minutes to be washed down.

NIGHT CRAWLER. West of Madera, the blind fingers of a harvester pick the vines clean.

going to run all day,

ONWARD. Moving at a speed of ½ mph, the machine handles much like a very slow tractor.

QUICK WORK. United Vintners' Mission Bell winery crushed all of these grapes between 1 and 3 p.m.

The big crush

A few years back, California winemakers
looked shamefacedly at long lines of
trucks waiting to unload their grapes into
crushers at big San Joaquin Valley
wineries. The lines meant all-day waits
while the grapes grew too warm under the
valley sun.

Bigger, more efficient equipment has
solved the problem. A new crusher
can handle 24 tons of grapes in 10 minutes.
At wineries with two to six crushers,
no truck is likely to wait more than three
hours.

ON DECK. Waiting in line is still waiting in line.

RUSH HOUR. Signal lights distribute trucks among the crushers.

Struggling to stay small

One measure of the San Joaquin Valley's size lies in the fact that a winery with 2 million gallons capacity is in truth among the small ones. Capacities do go lower—all the way down to 40,000 gallons—but only in a few rare instances.

The secret of small-scale survival in this valley of giants is specialized winemaking. It takes several forms.

One method is to make traditional, wood-aged table wines to compete with wines from the coast counties rather than the big neighbors. The basis is grape varieties developed specifically for valley climates by the University of California. In Lodi, for example, the Dino Barengo and East-Side wineries have capitalized on the UC grape called Ruby Cabernet with red wines that compete successfully against traditional varietals  grown in cooler climates. The acreages planted to these university-developed grapes are relatively small, but increasing at a rapid rate. Ruby Cabernet acreage alone grew from 2,374 in 1969 to 9,865 in 1972. All but a handful of these vines grow in the San Joaquin Valley.

Another survival technique is to concentrate on making one wine very well. Ficklin Vineyards is the premier example with its Tinta Port, as described on the facing page, but there are others. A small new winery called Landis specializes similarly in Sherry, and the emphasis at the Golden State Winery is on sparkling wines.

Finally, there is the country winery serving a local clientele with genuine *vin ordinaire*. True *ordinaire* is home-made wine, or a very accurate imitation of it, and can be had only in the neighborhood where it is made. There is a definite kinship between such valley wineries as Cadlolo, Farnesi, and Nonini and similar enterprises in Portugal, Spain, or Italy.

SPIRITS STORAGE ROOM

SATISFACTION. One of the rewards for making fine Port comes on a raw winter day when an excuse arises for opening one of the 1948s, and it still warms the soul. Dave Ficklin enjoys that privilege.

Tucked away at the end of an uncertain road southwest of Madera is a small winery which specializes to the ultimate degree. Its name is Ficklin Vineyards, and its only commercial product is Port.

The Ficklin family embarked on Port-making in the 1940s, partly in response to a University of California challenge to import and grow in California the grape varieties used to make Port in its original home, the Douro River Valley in Portugal. With traditional methods and grapes called Tinta Madeira, Tinta Cao, Alvarelhao, Touriga and Souzao, they produce a wine with a fame all out of proportion to the volume of production. The winery crushes a scant 70 tons of these grapes in a good vintage.

THE BOSS. Reno Nonini, second generation of his family to run the winery, is busy figuring out how to modernize his fermenting capacity.

DEMIJOHNS FOR SALE. At Cadlolo, the five-gallon demijohn full of Burgundy is a standard measure of trade with veteran customers who see no point in small bottles.

Serving the neighborhood

Before Prohibition, the Big Valley was full of little family wineries devoted to neighborhood trades. Some of them even loaded barrels onto wagons or trucks and made delivery rounds, much in the way small town dairies used to do. At this point there are no more than half a dozen of these wineries left in the whole of the San Joaquin. Nonini, west of Fresno, does a brisk business with local Basque restaurants and with regular customers who bring their own barrels in for filling. Farnesi, on the other side of town, occupies a similar niche. In the Escalon-Ripon area, Cadlolo and T. R. Hat share the family trade.

BIG AS A HOUSE. A 30,000-gallon tank made of redwood measures 14 feet across and nearly 20 feet high. Washing one requires a high-pressure hose and several hundred gallons of water. Barengo Cellars in Lodi is one of several wineries in the area with sizeable cellars full of such tanks.

THE KNACK. A veteran cellarman at Barengo slips into a tank with practiced ease.

HANDIWORK. Ancient hand-corking machine is good enough to drive 2,000 corks a day when the automatic bottling line breaks down, which automatic lines will do from time to time.

Getting into it

Every time a wine tank empties, a cellarman has to go inside to clean it. The essence of getting in is to climb a step just outside the manhole, lean, and do something very much like the first half of a butterfly stroke in swimming. Once his shoulders clear the portal, the cellarman must wriggle his lower half inward until one knee clears the gate so that he can get a leg inside to stand on. Going out, the process reverses itself: he sticks one leg out, then the other, then wriggles backwards until his waist can bend outside the tank.

BARE BONES. In winter, pruned vines reveal their basic structure. These vines are spur-pruned.

Training the grapes

Because so many grape varieties are grown for so many purposes in the San Joaquin Valley, the region is a sprawling textbook in the methods of pruning grape vines.

Basically there are two ways to prune: spur and cane. However, training and support methods expand the possibilities into the dozens. The choices are governed by climate (shelter the fruit in hot places, or expose it to the sun more in cool ones) and by purpose (work for a relatively large yield to make inexpensive blend wines, or a small crop to make expensive varietals that must be concentrated to have distinctive character).

HEAD TRAINED. The cupped shape formed by heavy arms (top photo) characterizes head trained vines. This is an ancient training technique for wine grapes, now disappearing from California and the rest of the world because it makes the fruit susceptible to disease and hard to pick. The vine is spur pruned.

SPUR PRUNED. Stubby spurs growing up from two or more heavy arms characterizes this method (middle photo), which allows trellising but is very hard on the vine. Trellising spreads the fruit out, reducing damage and difficulty.

CANE PRUNED. Long slim arms running along trellis wires (bottom photo) are the sign of cane pruning, now the favored method in California because of its flexibility. Each year, the old fruit-bearing cane is pruned away and a new one replaces it on the trellis wire, which means the plant may be completely re-shaped if need be.

As the twig is bent

California has two schools of grape growing and wine-making. One is at the University of California at Davis, the other at California State University at Fresno.

Although there is considerable overlap, Davis and Fresno are not exactly twins. The Department of Viticulture and Enology at UC-Davis a few miles west of Sacramento has become internationally famous among winemakers and wine drinkers alike as a center of research into vines and wines. The counterpart department at CSU-Fresno has a reputation within the wine industry based on its practical training of vineyardists.

"Practical training" amounts to more than the words suggest. Viticulture students learn how to drive tractors, prune vines, and lay out vineyards. They also learn plant genetics, entomology, and chemistry. Similarly, enology students learn how to couple hoses, hook up filters, and shovel pomace as one side of their studies, and they learn bacteriology, microbiology, and chemistry as the other side.

Although research programs frequently sound esoteric, research and practical application seldom stray far apart. In effect, the model vineyards grow half a plot according to the conventional wisdom and the other half by some untried method. The model wineries make wine the same way.

As a result, California growers not only know that Cabernet Sauvignon grapes from a hot place will not make good wine, they also know what goes wrong in the plant. As a result, they have hybrid varieties based on Cabernet Sauvignon that will grow in a hot place and still make good wine.

The winemakers know from University research which aromatic compounds give Cabernet Sauvignon its distinctive aroma and bouquet and which ways to ferment and age the wine in order to preserve optimum amounts of the good ones.

The same sort of experiments have been going on across the spectrum of wine types since 1875, when a legendary scholar named Eugene Waldemar Hilgard first involved the University in grapes and wine. His successors have yet to lay down the cudgels. Their students permeate the state's commercial vineyards and wineries.

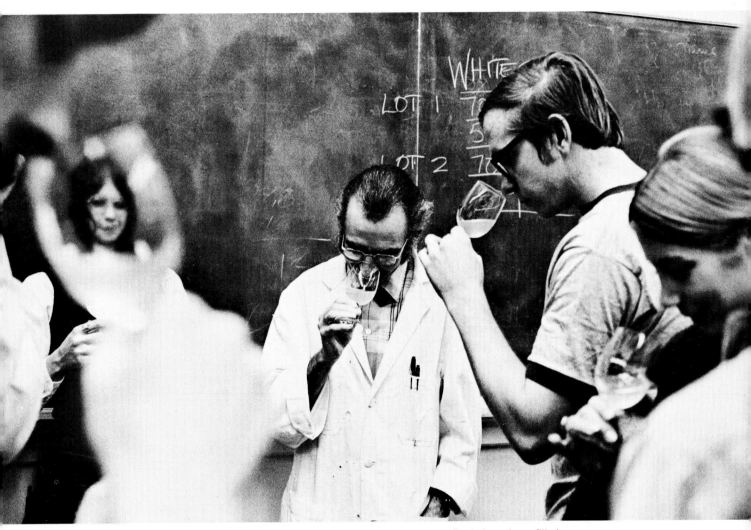

YOUTH WILL BE SERVED. Enology courses at the University of California at Davis have been filled to overflowing by the growing interest of Americans in wine. Professor A. D. Webb (in a lab coat) demonstrates the effects of varying levels of acid in white wine to an advanced class. Analytical tasting is as vital as analytical chemistry.

...As the twig is bent

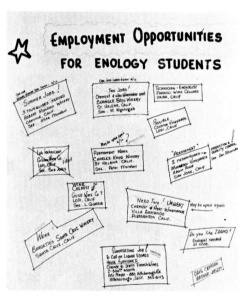

THE REAL REPORT CARD

THE CHOICE. At
CSU-Fresno, Professor
Vincent Petrucci instructs
a viticulture class in how
to look for canes with
superior potential to bear
fruit, the essence
of pruning.

TOOLS OF THE TRADE. Students in a UC-Davis class in enology learn from Professor Curtis Alley how to measure for sugar in grapes using a refractometer.

APPLIED WISDOM. Fresno students have a go at a cane-pruned vine in the university vineyard.

THE EXPERIMENTAL LIFE. Professor Harold Berg (below) is just finding out that one otherwise ideal vineyard weedicide hangs around, making wine from the treated vines taste like garlic. His Davis colleagues (left to right: Cornelius Ough, James Guymon and Vernon Singleton) already knew. They and Professor Maynard Amerine (at right) contributed many of the 13,000 experimental wines in the University's cellar, including the garlicky one.

NATURE'S ASSOCIATE. Professor H. P. Olmo directs UC programs in developing new grape varieties for wine and other use. To see how new plants are faring, assistant Billie Little counts every berry, aborted berry, seed, and other product of thousands of vines.

The fruits of research

Nature, in her own sweet time, will modify vines transplanted from one climate to another so they will grow well in their new homes. A man with a fine understanding of genetics and a lot of time can hasten the process immeasurably. In 30 years, Dr. H. P. Olmo of UC-Davis has grown some 225,000 crosses between two or more of the classic European varieties of *Vitis vinifera*, always seeking to develop new varieties attuned to California sun and soil.

In an average year he takes the grapes from each of 1,900 plants and makes 1,900 wines—about a half-bottle of each. These he tastes. Promising wines lead to further tries in the vineyard.

From this program have come increasingly familiar grape names: Emerald Riesling, Flora, Ruby Cabernet, Royalty, and Rubired. Emerald Riesling and Ruby Cabernet, especially, have prospered as purely California varietal table wines. Now, there is about to appear a new generation, led by a red grape called Carnelian, that seems likely to improve upon the best of these earlier successes.

Wine in the Gold Country

All California wine owes a great deal to the 1849 Gold Rush. It attracted many of the early winemakers and most of the pioneer population base. Although these indirect contributions are its greatest ones, the Gold Country also has a vinous past and present of its own.

At the turn of the Century, vineyards around the town of Coloma were yielding half a million gallons of wine and brandy a year. Other vines near the Amador County town of Plymouth were of similar scope.

The major concentration of vineyards in the Sierra foothills today is east of Plymouth in a shallow dip called the Shenandoah Valley. Most of the 600 acres in the region is planted to Zinfandel, which grows so well on these slopes that parts of the crop are exported to Napa and Santa Clara Counties to be made into wine there. Many of the grapes that stay home go to d'Agostini, a family winery with roots reaching back to 1856. A sizeable proportion goes to Montevina, a new winery in 1973.

To the north, Coloma is at the beginning of a small revival. So far it amounts to 37 acres and the tiny Gold Hill winery.

LOCAL COLOR. The Amador Winery in Amador City is one of several wine cellar-tasting rooms in the Gold Country.

NEW HOPE. Beverly Hempt runs a tasting room in Coloma. Husband John operates their tiny winery a few miles away.

THE CORNERSTONE. East of Plymouth, the d'Agostini winery has survived Prohibition, frost, and other calamities, keeping the Shenandoah Valley vineyards alive in the process.

TAKING WINE SERIOUSLY. Wine does not have to be a hobby. It can be nothing more than an unaffected mealtime beverage. However, it comes in so many forms that people can and do make it a lifetime study. The trick for serious tasters is to develop a detailed memory for what they have tasted and a sure understanding of the standards behind the many names of wines.

An
Appendix
for
Wine
Drinkers

Lessons on the labels

State and federal laws require labels on California wine bottles to explain a good deal about what is inside. Reading the fine print is almost always worthwhile.

① The trademark is a general statement of style, the signature of the company that made the wine. Some wineries maintain two or more labels to indicate wines of differing price, style, or origin.

② A vintage date can appear only if 95% or more of the grapes used to make the wine were harvested during the year stated. (The margin allows winemakers to top up casks with younger or older wines.)

Vintages do vary to a considerable degree in California. The primary point of concern to hobbyists is how the red wines of a certain year will age.

③ Every wine must carry some statement of geographic origin. For a wine to be called "California," all of the grapes in it must be grown and fermented within the state. (If a label reads "American" some of the grapes came from elsewhere.) For a wine to carry a more specific appellation, at least 75% of the grapes in it must be grown in the district named in the case of non-vintage-dated wines, or 95% in the case of vintage-dated ones. District appellations in common use in California are: North Coast (from grapes grown in any of the counties surrounding San Francisco, usually from several), Cucamonga, Livermore, Napa, Sonoma and Santa Clara. Any county name can be used as an appellation provided that the county has substantial grape acreage.

④ The name of a wine can be varietal, generic or proprietary.

A varietal is made at least 51% (usually 75 to 100%) from the namesake grape variety.

Generics have no legal requirement as to grapes used to make them. The idea is that the wines bear a relation-ship in character to wines made in the region from which the names are drawn.

Proprietaries are privately owned names, usually variations on the generic names.

The names used to describe California wines other than proprietaries are listed in the dictionary of wines that begins on the facing page.

⑤ As a minimum, the label must carry the name of the company that bottled the wine and the location of its cellars or offices, and the words "Bottled by." (It used to be the practice that the bottler would list the location of his bottling plant, but several firms now use only the site of their business headquarters.)

Cellared and bottled by, aged and bottled by, and perfected and bottled by; these are phrases to indicate that the bottler aged the wine on his premises to his own satisfaction.

Made and bottled by indicates that the bottler has crushing and fermenting facilities, and that he makes at least 10% of his own wine, perhaps as much as 70%.

Produced and bottled by indicates that the bottler crushes and ferments 75% or more of his own wine.

⑥ The percentage of alcohol is a good index to the type of wine. Table wines are permitted to range between 10% and 14% alcohol; the exact content can vary ½% on either side of the figure stated on the label. If the alcohol total is between 17% and 20%, the wine has been fortified by the addition of grape brandy. If the figure is between 7% and 10%, or between 14% and 17%, chances are that the beverage has been flavored with something other than grapes. If there is any added material, the fine print on the label must specify the fact.

A Dictionary of California Wines

The following dictionary describes all of the generic and varietal names commonly used to identify California wines. Pronunciations are Anglicized approximations of the original French, German, and Italian words based upon a guide originally developed by The Wine Institute of California.

Aleatico. *(Ah lay ATTIC oh)* A varietal sometimes made as a sweet table wine, sometimes as a fortified dessert wine. It is rare in either case and reserved for dessert sipping in both.

The grape, imported from Italy, is related to the Muscats. It shares their pronounced family flavor.

Alicante Bouschet. *(Ah lee CANT Boo shay)* Appears on rare occasion as a varietal red table wine. Most Alicante grapes disappear into Burgundy blends to add color. The tough-skinned fruit ships well, so is also a staple in the home winemaking market.

The grape came originally from Spain.

Angelica. *(Ahn JELL ee cah)* Originally made by mixing brandy with fresh grape juice, it is now made either as a brandy-fortified dessert wine or—by sacramental wineries—as a natural sweet white wine. The fortified bottlings, tawny in color and sweet to taste, much resemble cream Sherries. The lower alcohol Angelicas are white, somewhat kindred to "Chateau" wines or Haut Sauternes.

Traditionally, Angelicas of either type are made from Mission grapes, but no law limits varieties that may be used.

Appetizer wine. A term which describes a whole class of relatively dry wines with alcohol contents raised to 17 to 20% by the addition of grape brandy. Beyond these similarities, the wines may differ widely. The principal type is dry or cocktail Sherry. Madeira is a variation. Both depend upon aging in warmth for their characteristic flavors. Another type is white Vermouth, which depends instead on infusions of herbs and spices for its individual flavor.

Barbera. *(Bar BAIR ah)* A varietal red table wine, Barbera is full-bodied, dry, tannic, strongly vinous to taste. Bottlings from North Coast vineyards often show ability to age up to 10 years. Young, the wine frequently accompanies pasta or seafood stews in spicy tomato sauces. As Barbera ages, it becomes a favorite with game, especially venison.

The grape variety has its origins in Italy's Piedmont. Italian family wineries in Napa, Sonoma and Santa Clara make most of the varietal Barbera in California.

Black Muscat. *(MUSS cat)* A ruby-colored dessert wine made from one of the black-skinned members of the Muscat family of grapes. Sweet, with an alcohol content between 17 and 20%, it may be regarded as a grapey tasting alternative to Ruby Port.

Blanc de Blancs. *(Blonh de blonh)* The phrase means white wine made from white grapes. For the most part it serves as a descriptive on Champagnes made to be light in style, although there is at least one white table wine so named. There is no legal limit on which white grapes may be used to make a wine of this name.

Blanc de Noir. *(Blonh de nwahr)* The phrase means white wine made from black grapes. As in the case of Blanc de Blancs it applies primarily to Champagnes, usually ones made from Pinot noir grapes.

Blanc Fumé. *(Blonh Few MAY)* A varietal white table wine, Blanc Fumé is almost always dry. Some connoisseurs say the taste of the grape reminds them of herbaceous or grassy flavors. Others say the taste is smoky. In any case, the flavor is pronounced, making the wine an excellent companion to well-seasoned poultry dishes.

The name is drawn from the Loire Valley in France, where the grape is used to make the wine called Pouilly

Fumé. The same grape or a closely related one grows in the Sauternes and Graves districts of France as Sauvignon Blanc. The California grape is Sauvignon Blanc. Wines from it are known by both names plus several variations. (See: Sauvignon Blanc.)

Brut Champagne. *(Broo Sham PAIN)* Champagne is in the United States a generic word for white or pink sparkling wine. Brut means the wine is white, quite dry. Further, the word is a practical guarantee that the wine is bottle-fermented. Being dry, Brut is a classic companion to first courses at formal meals. There is no limitation on grape varieties. (See: Champagne.)

Burgundy. A generic red table wine of widely varying character and style, ranging from dry to rather sweet, from light to full-bodied, and from pale crimson to dark, purplish red in color. The basic distinction is price. Inexpensive Burgundies, especially those bottled in the San Joaquin Valley, tend toward the fuller, sweeter end of the scale. More expensive bottles from North Coast Counties wineries generally are lighter and drier. In either case Burgundies are the American equivalent of French *vin ordinaire*, the wine meant to be drunk nightly as a flavorful lubricant to dinner rather than as a critical exercise in wine connoisseurship.

No regulation limits grape varieties that may be used, but Alicante Bouschet, Carignane, Petite Sirah, and Zinfandel loom large in most blends.

Cabernet. *(Cah bear NAY)* A semi-varietal red table wine made from grapes of the Cabernet family. Coined to cover early blends of Ruby Cabernet with other grapes, the label has nearly fallen out of use now that Ruby Cabernet has established an identity of its own. (See: Ruby Cabernet.)

Cabernet Sauvignon. *(Cah bear NAY So veen YONH)* At present the most prestigious of California's varietal red table wines, Cabernet Sauvignon is dry, full-bodied, highly distinctive. Its dominant characteristics as a young wine are tannin (the quality that makes cheeks pucker) and sharp flavors that remind experts more of herbs than fruit. Routinely capable of aging a decade, Cabernet Sauvignon develops a velvety complexity with time. As old wine, it is a frequent companion to beef or lamb prepared as classic French cuisine.

The grape was imported to California from the Bordeaux region of France, where it is the principal grape among several varieties blended to make the great chateau clarets of the Medoc.

Carignane. *(CARE een yanh)* A varietal red table wine, Carignane has only recently emerged from obscurity as a blend grape. The wine is heavy-bodied, tannic, a companion to spicy tomato sauces and other hearty country cooking.

The grape variety has its origins in the Mediterranean region of Europe.

Chablis. *(Shah BLEE)* The most widely available generic white table wine, it is almost always dry or nearly so. The essential point of its style is a light, clean, fruity flavor (which is sometimes more easily achieved with a hint of sweet as part of the makeup).

Chablis is meant to be an uncomplicated part of the nightly dinner table in the same way as Burgundy is among reds. Similarly, the basic distinction is price. Inexpensive Chablis, especially those bottled in the San Joaquin Valley, tend to be fuller and sweeter than those from North Coast wineries which focus their production on varietal wines.

In recent years there has been a tendency among the large wineries to add a modifying word to Chablis—usually Chablis Blanc or Gold Chablis—but the wine is the same.

No regulation limits the grape varieties that may be used, but some frequently used ones are Burger, Chenin Blanc, French Colombard, and Sauvignon Vert.

Champagne. *(Sham PAIN)* In the United States, Champagne is a generic word for white or pink sparkling wine. A wine labeled Champagne may be dry or sweet and may be made in one of three ways. The label is required by law to state the method used; habitually it will also note the degree of sweetness.

A label reading "methode champenoise" or "fermented in this bottle" indicates that the wine was made by the oldest and most painstaking method known (see page 112 for a schematic explanation). These are usually the highest priced wines, made from the finest grape varieties.

A label reading either "Bottle fermented" or "Transfer process" is fermented in the bottle. However, cost- and labor-saving machines that do away with much of the hand labor of methode champenoise also remove the wine from its original bottle and put it back into a large tank at one point.

A label reading "Charmat process" or "Bulk process" means that the wine was fermented not in individual bottles, but rather in sizeable tanks. Most of the inexpensive champagnes are made by this method.

The degree of sweetness is noted on the label by one of the following terms:

Natural—no sweetness at all.
Brut *(Brou)*—little or no sweetness.
Extra Dry—faintly sweet.
Sec *(Seck)*—the sweetest of American sparkling wines.
The drier Champagnes can be used as elegant appetizers to formal meals, or as the wine with a notably

festive meal. Extra Dry is the versatile middle ground, soft enough to be enjoyable with festive meals or as a party beverage. Sec is sweet enough to be at its best as a dessert capping a memorable occasion.

Charbono. *(Shar BONE oh)*   A varietal red table wine which is offered only by Inglenook. The grape variety is Italian by origin. It makes a full-bodied, tannic red somewhat along the lines of Barbera but varietally distinct from it.

Chardonnay. *(Shar done NAY)*   A varietal white wine, the counterpart to Cabernet Sauvignon in prestige among California wines. Wine hobbyists characterize Chardonnay as austere. Some say its flavor is faintly reminiscent of apples. In any case, it is frequently called upon to temper the buttery riches of lobster, or dishes served in elegant but rich cream sauces. Chardonnay is one of very few white wines aged for long periods in small oak barrels, as many red wines are. Once bottled, a fine Chardonnay may age for six or eight years.

The grape is that of the great white Burgundies of France.

Chateau _____. *(Shah TOE)*   The word "Chateau" is always followed by a winery name (Chateau LaSalle, Chateau Beaulieu) or a grape name (Chateau Semillon). A generic white wine, it is always sweet. In effect, "Chateau" is an alternate label for Haut Sauterne.

Chenin Blanc. *(Cheh NANH Blonh)*   A varietal white table wine, usually sweet enough to teeter on the border between being good for dinner and better for dessert. Dry wine from the same grape usually is labeled as White Pinot or Pineau. Then it is an agreeably light and fruity wine with poultry or shellfish. Sweeter, Chenin Blanc goes well with luncheons or picnics.

The grape had its origins in the Loire River Valley of France, where it is a major element in Vouvrays.

Chianti. *(KEY auntie)*   A generic red table wine patterned not after the original Italian Chianti but after a more general model of Italian everyday red wine. California Chiantis are infallibly full-bodied but thereafter vary considerably. Those from the Central Valley are typically soft and faintly sweet. Those from the North Coast counties tend toward a sharper, drier character. Both are intended to mate well with pasta, pizza, and anything with tomato sauce on it.

There is no limit on grape varieties that may be used.

Claret. *(CLAIRE et)*   A generic red table wine, it is not offered by many producers now. In theory it is a lighter, more delicate wine than Burgundy, but in practice is very difficult to distinguish from it. (See: Burgundy.)

Cocktail Sherry.   A medium dry to dry Sherry suited to use as an appetizer or snack wine with nuts, crackers,

black olives, and the like. The alcohol ranges between 17 and 20%. (See: Sherry.)

Cold Duck.   A sparkling wine, pale red in color, that is almost always sweet and must taste clearly of the native American Concord grape to be true to its type. (Concord is the broad flavor in grape juice, grapeade, etc. . . . the flavor most Americans know as "grapey.") Cold Duck has done much to remove sparkling wine from the festive event-only image of Champagnes. Most Cold Ducks sell at a price to encourage casual drinking at picnics or at ordinary mid week dinners.

Crackling Rosé. *(Roe ZAY)*   A pink wine that sparkles somewhat less vigorously than Pink Champagne because it is fermented in a different way. Crackling Rosé is otherwise much like a Pink Champagne: a bit sweet, fruity, a good wine to have with a luncheon or picnic.

Cream Sherry.   The sweetest of California Sherries, usually with 20% alcohol, always best served with a light dessert or instead of a rich one. (See: Sherry.)

Dessert wine.   A term which describes a whole class of obviously sweet wines with alcohol contents raised to 17 to 20% by the addition of grape brandy. The principal type is Port. Others include Malvasia, Marsala, Muscatel and Tokay.

There is semantic confusion. Dessert wine, legally, must be fortified by the addition of brandy to bring its alcohol to the stated levels. Wines of 12% alcohol may be too sweet for any use other than dessert, but their legal status is table wine because the technical definition is based upon alcohol content, not sugar content.

Dry Muscat. *(MUSS cat)*   A semi-varietal white table wine, Dry Muscat is made mostly by small country wineries for local trade. The wine is a traditional part of Italian family dinner tables. Marked by the Muscat family flavor, its faintly bitter aftertaste is held by its devotees to be just right with Italian home cooking.

Dry Sauterne. *(So TAIRN)*   A generic white table wine. The word dry is the winemaker's guarantee that the wine is meant to go with a meal rather than as dessert. (See: Sauterne.)

Dry Sherry.   Usually a medium dry to dry Sherry suited to use as an appetizer. The word dry is more or less interchangeable with cocktail as an indication of relative dryness. (See: Sherry.)

Emerald Riesling. *(REEZ ling)* A varietal white table wine, light, fresh, usually with just a hint of sweet. The fruit flavors are recognizably related to other varieties of the Riesling family. Emerald Riesling is used, much as its cousins are, with shellfish and poultry.

The grape is one of those developed by the University of California at Davis to allow the making of dry table wines in the warmer regions of the San Joaquin Valley. Its parents are Johannisberg Riesling and Muscadelle, one of the Muscat family.

Extra Dry. Extra Dry on a bottle of sparkling wine means that the wine is not quite dry but rather fruity enough and soft enough to be agreeable with luncheons, bon voyage parties, and other festive meals. (See: Champagne.)

Fino. *(FEE no)* The word Fino indicates a light, dry Sherry with about 17% alcohol. The style of Fino is to retain fruity flavors rather than strike for pronounced tastes of oxidation. (See: Sherry.)

Flor. The word Flor on a label indicates that a light, dry Sherry has been flavored by a specific strain of yeast that grows naturally on Sherries in Spain. In California Flor is cultivated as a floating film after the Spanish fashion or is stirred into the wine during the aging process. (See: Sherry.)

Flora. A varietal white table wine from yet another of the varieties developed by the University of California. Flora is descended from Traminers, has a flavor faintly reminiscent of them, is usually slightly sweet, and is meant for light luncheon meals, picnics, or leisurely sipping on summer afternoons.

Folle Blanche. *(Foal Blonsh)* A varietal white table wine made only by Louis M. Martini in California, Folle Blanche is a light, clean, dry wine. As such, it is versatile enough for daily table use with all fish and poultry and with many casseroles or other delicately flavored foods.

The grape had its origins in the Cognac district of France, where it was used to make brandies until largely supplanted a few decades ago.

French Colombard. *(Coll om BARD)* A varietal white table wine from a grape with an unusually perfumey character. It has emerged as a varietal in recent years after long and honorable duty as a blend grape for Chablis, Sauternes, and other generics. Because of its aromatic qualities, French Colombard often is chosen with well-seasoned poultry dishes.

Fumé Blanc. *(Few MAY Blonh)* A varietal white table wine. The name is a variant of Blanc Fumé. (See: Blanc Fumé.)

Gamay. *(Gah MAY)* A varietal red table wine, Gamay is usually light, fresh, the fruitiest of the red wines. Most Gamays are meant to be consumed within a year or two with everyday dinners. This is especially true if the label also calls the wine Vivace *(Vee VOSS)* or Nouveau *(Noo VO)*.

The Gamay variety originated in the Burgundy region of France. It dominates the wine of Beaujolais there. In California, there are two grapes called Gamay. One is the Gamay or Napa Gamay, which is a true Gamay of Beaujolais. The other is the Gamay Beaujolais which—in spite of its name—is a sub-variety of Pinot Noir.

Gamay Beaujolais. *(Gah MAY Bo jo LAY)* A varietal red table wine, light and fresh in style, much like a wine simply labeled Gamay.

It comes from the grape called Gamay Beaujolais in California. For a note on the confused names of Gamay grapes, see Gamay.

Gamay Noir. *(Gah MAY N'wahr)* A varietal red table wine made from the same grape as Gamay. (See: Gamay.)

Gamay Rosé. *(Gah MAY Roe ZAY)* A varietal pink table wine, fresh, slightly sweet, Gamay is made from the same grape variety as Gamay.

Gewürztraminer. *(Geh WIRTS trah meen err)* A varietal white table wine with a pronounced spicy characteristic, it is so pungent in flavor that many people prefer to drink the wine with appetizers—especially pâtés—rather than as accompaniment to a meal. Most Gewürztraminers have a faint touch of sweet about them to round them out as wines for appetizer sipping.

The grape variety was brought to California from the French province of Alsace where Gewürztraminers are used both as appetizer and accompaniment to *choucroute garni*.

Green Hungarian. A varietal white table wine, Green Hungarians are usually light, fresh, and not quite dry.

The grape is made as a varietal by only a few wineries. Most of the crop is blended into Chablis.

Grenache. *(Gren AHSH)*   A varietal red table wine on rare occasion. The grape is so strong in flavor and pale in color that most of the crop is made into Rosé.

Grenache Rosé. *(Gren AHSH Rose AY)*   A varietal pink table wine, the dominant one in California. Grenache grapes impart a strongly perfumey character to red wine but a tempered one to rosés. Almost always noticeably sweet, Grenache Rosés are often served with ham or other pork or at picnics or luncheons.

The grape was imported to California from the Tavel region of France, where the wines are made drier and aged longer than in this country.

Grey Riesling. *(REEZ ling)*   A varietal white table wine, light, fresh, delicate in character, almost always slightly sweet. The wine is versatile with poultry, white fish, and picnic fare.

The grape variety originated in France, where it is usually known as Chauché gris. The name Grey Riesling arose in California for undefinable reasons.

Grignolino. *(Green yo LEEN oh)*   A varietal red table wine of unusually tart, piquant character, Grignolino is made by only a few California wineries. Its sharp, cleansing capacities make it an excellent companion to lamb or other rich meat dishes. Grignolinos usually are made to be drunk young.

The grape variety is north Italian in origin.

Haut Sauterne. *(Oh So TAIRN)*   A generic white table wine. The word Haut is synonymous in California with sweet. (See: Sauterne.)

Johannisberg Riesling. *(Yo HAN iss bairg REEZ ling)*   A varietal white table wine made to emphasize the piquantly fresh fruity flavor of the grape. Almost always marked by a faint hint of sweet, Johannisberg is regarded by its admirers as the quintessential accompaniment to clams, crab, shrimp, or other seafood dishes. Because of

its fruity nature, Johannisberg from California is almost always preferred as a very young wine.

The grape variety originated in Germany, where it is the dominant variety in wines of the Rheingau and Mosel. Its true botanic name in California is White Riesling. A few wineries bottle their wine under this name.

Kleinberger Riesling. *(KLYN bairg er REEZ ling)*   A varietal white table wine made only by Sebastiani in California, and only occasionally by them. The wine is light, delicate of flavor, recommendable with unadorned chicken.

The grape variety is a rather distant relation of the white Riesling grape, little grown either in Germany or California.

Madeira. *(Mah DARE ah)*   A white appetizer wine, slightly sweet, and oxidized to produce a characteristic nutty flavor and tawny color. Only Paul Masson produces a wine under this name in California at present, although most California Sherries are made more in the fashion of the original Madeiras than the original Sherries. (Madeira is an island possession of Portugal; Sherry is wine from the Xeres district of Spain.) Madeiras are made by exposing fortified white wine to heat and air. Sherries do not use the heat. (See: Sherry.)

Malvasia Bianca. *(Mahl ve ZEE ah Bee AHN ca)*   A white wine from one of the Muscat family of grapes, sometimes made with 12% alcohol as a table wine, sometimes at 20% as a pure dessert wine. Both styles are usually sweet, marked by relatively delicate family flavor of Muscat. A few wineries make Malvasia as a sparkling wine patterned on the Asti Spumantes of Italy. The variety was imported to California from the Asti region.

Marsala. *(Mar SAH lah)*   A generic dessert wine made rather rarely in California, Marsala is very sweet. The color is dark amber. Most Marsalas taste surprisingly like raisins. The flavor is imparted by using very ripe grapes, frequently Missions and Grenache. Because of its intensely sweet flavor, it lends itself to sipping in small amounts.

Merlot. *(Mare LOW)* A varietal red table wine, Merlot bears some resemblance to Cabernet Sauvignon in flavor but is softer in character. It is not widely planted and has only recently emerged as a varietal.

The grape comes from the Bordeaux region of France where it is a minor part of wines from the great Chateaux of the Medoc, but a major factor in the wines of St. Emilion and Pomerol.

Moscato Canelli. *(Moe SCOT oh Cah NELLY)* A white varietal table wine, Moscato is made sweet enough to go more readily with dessert than a meal. The wine tastes markedly of the Muscat family flavor without being as coarse as many of its cousins.

The grape grows widely in Italy and France. The French know it as Muscat Frontignan.

Muscat Frontignan. *(MUSS cat Frawn teen YANH)* A varietal white dessert wine in California, Muscat Frontignan is very fruity in youth but capable of aging into an elegant old wine.

Mountain Red. A generic red table wine, Mountain Red is made in the same way and from the same grapes as Burgundy. In effect, the name is an effort to get away from using European names to describe California wines. The virtuous effort has not overcome consumer preference for the name Burgundy. (See: Burgundy.)

Mountain White. A generic white table wine bearing the same relationship to Chablis as Mountain Red does to Burgundy. (See: Mountain Red, Chablis.)

Muscatel. *(MUSS cah tell)* A semi-varietal dessert wine, always quite sweet. There are many grape varieties within the Muscat family, all sharing a distinct flavor. There are variations of flavor from one grape to another, so Muscatels may vary slightly from one winery to another depending on the blend. They are the "grapiest" of all dessert wines, which is to say they taste most nearly like fresh grapes of any brandy-fortified wine.

Nebbiolo. *(Neh bee OH low)* A varietal red table wine made by only one winery, Cal Grape, under its H. O. Lanza label. The wine is dry, generally similar to San Joaquin Valley Barberas. (See: Barbera.)

In Italy's Piedmont, where the grape variety originated, Nebbiolo is the basis of most prestigious red wines of the region.

Natural. The designation for bone-dry Champagnes. (See: Champagne.)

Palomino. *(Pal oh MEEN oh)* A varietal Sherry, usually made rather dry as an apéritif wine in California.

The grape is the classic variety of fine Spanish Sherries. (See: Sherry.)

Pedro Ximinez. *(PAY dro Hee MEE nez)* A varietal Sherry, rarely made in California, always dessert sweet when it does appear.

The grape variety is thought to be a mutation of the German variety, White Riesling, grown in Spain. (See: Sherry.)

Petite Sirah. *(P'TEET Sear RAH)* A varietal red table wine, always dry, usually with enough tannin to be puckery. Like Barbera, it is a vinous red, well suited to heavy meals centered around well-seasoned meats.

The grape is one of several grown in the Rhone Valley of France. Recent evidence suggests that the California Sirah is not the true Sirah but rather a related variety called Duriff in France. Widely planted in California, it once was limited to use in Burgundy blends but recently has emerged as a varietal in its own right.

Pineau de la Loire. *(Pea NO d la l'wahr)* A varietal white table wine from a grape also known as Chenin Blanc and White Pinot. (See: Chenin Blanc.)

Pink Chablis. *(Shah BLEE)* A generic pink table wine, usually faintly sweet and marked by a hint of effervescence. Except for the hint of bubble, Pink Chablis is interchangeable with Vin Rosé. The name is a commercial coinage much frowned upon by connoisseurs of wine because no rosé is made in the namesake Chablis district of France, but the name is successful anyway.

No legal restriction limits grape varieties.

Pink Champagne. *(Sham PAIN)* A generic sparkling pink wine made by one of the three champagne methods. Most bottlings are somewhat sweet. The wine is usually reserved for festive brunches and similar occasions. No legal restriction limits grape varieties. (See: Champagne.)

Pinot Blanc. *(Pea NO Blonh)* A varietal white table wine, almost always dry, usually somewhat kindred to Chardonnay in character. For a variety of reasons it is slowly disappearing as a variety.

The grape is secondary to Chardonnay in the Burgundy region of France.

Pinot Chardonnay. *(Pea NO Shar done NAY)* A varietal white table wine, the usual label in California for wine from a grape with the true name of Chardonnay. (See: Chardonnay.)

Pinot Noir. *(Pea NO N'wahr)* Always dry, always delicate, it ranks second in prestige only to Cabernet Sauvignon among California varietal red table wines. Pinot Noir, considerably less tannic than Cabernet, matures more quickly, in three to five years. Its softness makes it a favored wine with steak and other beef dishes.

Pinot Noir is the principal grape of the great red Burgundies of France.

Pinot St. George. *(Pea NO Sant Jorge)* A varietal red wine kindred to Pinot Noir but less defined in character. Rather rare in California, it is an agreeable companion to all red meats.

The grape is a secondary variety in the Burgundy districts of France.

Port. A generic term used to cover a wide range of dessert wines. Port is made by adding brandy to a must while the fermentation is in progress. The effect is to stop the fermentation and raise the alcohol level to about 20%. The brandy is added at the moment when unfermented grape sugar will result in a wine of predetermined sweetness.

Ruby Ports are made from red grapes, especially Zinfandel, Mataro and Royalty; Tawny Ports are from a blend of red and white grape varieties; White Ports are from white varieties, frequently of the Muscat family. The only varietal or semi-varietal Port is Tinta, a ruby type from Tinta Madeira and other Portuguese grapes.

Red Pinot. *(Pea NO)* A varietal red table wine. The name is a seldom-used synonym for Pinot St. George. (See: Pinot St. George.)

Rhine. A generic white table wine, usually but not always made with a sweet edge in the style of Liebfraumilchs, Moselblumchens, and similar inexpensive wines of Germany. Most large California producers offer Rhine as a sweeter alternative to their Chablis or Dry Sauterne. A few smaller ones offer a wine of this name as a drier alternative to their Chablis. The wine goes well with picnic chicken and similar dishes.

No legal limitation controls grape varieties that may be used.

Riesling. *(REEZ ling)* A semi-varietal white table wine made from blends of grapes in the Riesling family. The wines are almost always faintly sweet, light, and fruity, meant to accompany such dishes as steamed clams, cracked crab, and fried chicken. The usual base grape in a Riesling blend is Sylvaner. (See: Sylvaner.)

Rosé of Cabernet Sauvignon. *(Roe ZAY of Cah bear NAY So veen YONH)* A varietal pink table wine, rarely made in California but almost certain to be the driest of pink wines when it is and one of the most distinctively flavored. It is of such firm character that it goes very well with barbecued steaks. (See: Cabernet Sauvignon.)

Royalty. A varietal red table wine, rarely made, usually sweet. Most Royalty is sipped for itself. It is from a grape developed by the University of California to grow in the San Joaquin Valley as a base for Port-type wines.

Ruby Cabernet. *(Cah bear NAY)* A varietal red table wine, Ruby Cabernet is one of the first commercially successful varieties developed by the University of California to grow in warm San Joaquin Valley conditions. The wine is usually dry, noticeably related in grape flavor to Cabernet Sauvignon. It is frequently served with beef or other red meats.

The parents of Ruby Cabernet are Cabernet Sauvignon (for character and finesse) and Carignane (for heat tolerance and ability to bear sizeable crops).

Ruby Port. A generic red dessert wine, always sweet, made to go with nuts, pound cake, or a book by the fire. No legal restriction limits grape varieties that may be used, but Mataro, Royalty, and Zinfandel are the bases of many Ruby Ports. (See: Port.)

Sauterne. *(So TAIRN)* A generic white table wine. Individual bottles range from very dry to very sweet. The dry ones are usually labelled just Sauterne, sometimes Dry Sauterne. Sweet ones are usually labelled Haut Sauterne. In general, Dry Sauterne and Chablis are interchangeable names on inexpensive white wines. Sometimes relatively expensive bottlings labelled Dry Sauterne carry a subtitle, Semillon, which means they are in fact a varietal. (See: Semillon.) The sweet bottlings are meant to be used with dessert. (See: Haut Sauterne.)

Sauvignon Blanc. *(So veen YONH Blonh)* A varietal white table wine from one of the principal grapes of the Sauternes district in France. In California, the variety is used to make wines ranging from bone dry to very sweet. Wine from this grape goes by several aliases, including Blanc Fumé, Blanc de Sauvignon, Fumé Blanc, and in one case, Pouilly Fumé. (See: Blanc Fumé.)

The nomenclature is quite confusing at present, although there is a tendency toward using one of the "Fumé" names to identify the drier wines, and Sauvignon Blanc the sweeter ones.

In a dry wine, the flavor of this grape variety is intense, almost grassy in character, which causes dry Sauvignon Blancs and Fumés to be frequent accompaniment to highly seasoned poultry or seafood. Sweet, the wine from Sauvignon Blanc, is richly fruity, suited to after-dinner sipping with fresh fruit or plain pound cake.

Sauvignon Vert. *(So veen YONH Vair)* Rarely made as a varietal white wine. The grape is used mostly as a blend grape in generic whites, valued for its high acidity. As a varietal it is dry, rather muted in flavor, an agreeable companion to well-seasoned fish and poultry dishes.

Sec. *(Seck)* The word sec translates from French as "dry," but does not mean it. "Sec" on a label signifies the sweetest Champagne in the line produced by a particular winery. There is no precise legal requirement on the degree of sweetness, but it is always enough to use the wine as a dessert. (See: Champagne.)

Semillon. *(Say me YONH)* A varietal white table wine from the companion grape to Sauvignon Blanc in the Sauternes district of France. In California, Semillon is made as a dry wine more often than not but does appear as a sweet wine on occasion. Dry, it has an unusually distinctive perfumey flavor. Its admirers find it well suited to poultry dishes with cream sauces. The occasional sweet bottlings are well thought of as companions to fresh fruit.

Curiously, the name never has become popular, although people like the wine and buy it labelled as Sauterne.

Sherry. A generic term used to cover a wide range of appetizer and dessert wines.

In California, typical Sherries begin as white wines—dry ones for dry Sherries, sweet ones for dessert Sherries. These have grape brandy added to them, bringing the alcohol level to 17 to 20%. The fortified wines are then aged in about 110° of heat and also with a large surface exposed to the air. The heat and air together turn the wine at least to pale amber, usually to a definite brown color. The aging also produces an intense flavor most people think of as "nutty." This method resembles techniques used to make the Portuguese wines called Madeira more than those used to make Sherry in Spain. One Spanish technique used in California is flor, a yeast that is kept in contact with the wine as it ages to produce a distinctive yeasty flavor.

California Sherries dry enough to serve with appetizers are usually called Dry, Cocktail, Fino, Sack, or just plain "Sherry." Sweet ones for dessert are called Cream Sherry.

Sparkling Burgundy. A generic red sparkling wine, it must be produced by one of the accepted Champagne methods to earn the name. (See: Champagne.) Most Sparkling Burgundies are sweet in about the same degree as Extra Dry or Sec Champagne, but a few producers make this wine dry. It is normally used to accent the festive qualities of dinners celebrating weddings or anniversaries.

Sparkling wine. The name used to describe a whole class of wines with effervescence produced by a secondary fermentation in a closed container, which is to say by one of the methods for making Champagne. The class includes all white Champagnes, Pink Champagne, Sparkling Burgundy, and sparkling Muscats. It does not include wine with bubbles introduced by carbonation or any other method than secondary fermentation. (See: Champagne.)

St. Emilion. *(Sant Eh mee YONH)* A rarely made varietal white table wine. The name is a synonym for the main botanic name of the grape, Ugni Bianco. The wine is soft, somewhat like Chenin Blanc, and suited to poultry.

The grape variety has its origin in northern Italy.

Sylvaner. *(Sill VON er)* A varietal white table wine, almost always made with a faint tinge of sweet to accent its clean, fruity flavors. Some labels read Sylvaner, some Sylvaner-Riesling. It is the same wine in either case. The grape is a secondary one to White Riesling in Germany and in California. Although Sylvaner lacks the complexity and richness of flavor that mark White Riesling, it is a versatile companion to clams, fresh crab, white fish, poultry, and other light meats. It is much favored for luncheons and picnics because of its freshness.

Table wine. The name used to describe a whole class of wines naturally fermented to about 12% alcohol. The class includes all red, white, and pink wines with these qualities. The name derives from the primary use of these wines as mealtime accompaniments to food. Most are "dry," which is to say they have only a very small amount of unfermented sugar remaining—or none at all. Some are sweet enough to be used with dessert but retain their classification as table wine because percentage of alcohol is the tax base for wines, and wines of 10½ to 13½% alcohol are taxed as table wine no matter how sweet. (See: Dessert wine.)

Tawny Port. A generic red dessert wine. As a flavor, it offers a bridge between Cream Sherries and Ruby Ports.

Although no legal requirement limits grape varieties that may be used, most blends combine some white grapes with red grapes of low to moderate color in order to produce the faintly red, deeply tawny hue. It is sometimes thought that Tawny Ports are exceptionally old, but this is not the case either in California or Portugal. The choice of grapes establishes the pale color at the outset.

Tinta Port. *(TEEN ta)* A semi-varietal red dessert wine, usually made with a Portuguese grape called Tinta Madeira as the base. Other Portuguese red grapes may be included, such as Alvarelhao, Souzao, Tinta Cao, and Touriga.

In general character a Tinta is a Ruby Port, although with sharper definition of its fruity flavors than an average Ruby.

Traminer. *(Tra meen ERR)* A varietal white table wine, Traminer is made from a grape called the Veltliner, a close relation to the true Traminer grape. Wines sold under the name tend to be light, fruity, not quite dry. They go well with clams, white fish, poultry, and kindred foods.

The variety is from the French province of Alsace.

Vermouth. *(Ver MOOTH)* An appetizer wine, either white or red, flavored by an infusion of natural essences of herbs and spices. The formulas for these infusions are always commercial secrets of the proprietors.

White Vermouth is relatively dry. Red Vermouth is always quite sweet. Both can be enjoyed for themselves or used as a source of flavor in cocktails.

Vin Rosé. *(Van Roe ZAY)* A generic pink table wine, almost always made slightly sweet to accentuate its fruity flavors. Rosés go particularly well with ham and other pork. The broader purpose of the wine is to cheer up picnics, luncheons, or other informal meals.

No regulation limits the grape varieties that may be used.

Vino Rosso. *(VEE no ROE so)* A generic red table wine, always pronouncedly sweet, grapey, and full-bodied. The style is much favored among Italian families along the Atlantic seaboard as an accompaniment to hearty, home-style cooking. There are a number of variations on the name, including Vino da Pranza and Vino Pastoso, Vino Pastoso e Scelto.

No regulation limits the grape varieties that may be used.

White Burgundy. A generic white table wine, usually dry and rather crisp. No legal requirement limits the grape varieties that may be used. In effect, the name is an alternative to Chablis. (See: Chablis.)

White Pinot. *(Pea NO)* A varietal white table wine. The name is a mistaken early translation of Pineau de la Loire, a grape variety more widely known as Chenin Blanc. A wine labelled thus is usually drier than one called Chenin Blanc. (See: Chenin Blanc.)

White Port. A white dessert wine, always very sweet and made to accent the fresh fruity flavors of its grapes. For this reason, many white Ports taste clearly of Muscat grapes. It is a wine for sipping with a bowl of fruit.

White Riesling. *(REEZ ling)* A few wineries label a varietal white table wine as White Riesling, the correct American botanical name for the premier grape of Germany's Rhine and Mosel districts. However, most California wines made from the grape are labeled as Johannisberg Riesling after the famous Schloss Johannisberg in the Rheingau. (See: Johannisberg Riesling.)

Zinfandel. *(Zin fan DELL)* A varietal red table wine from the most widely planted grape in the state. The extreme range of plantings in turn yields an extreme range of Zinfandels. (See the Red Wine Chart on page 214.) Those from the cooler parts of the north coast counties typically are delicate, fresh wines in youth. Connoisseurs say the flavor brings berries to mind. From time to time these north coast Zinfandels are robust enough to age for 6 to 10 years.

Zinfandels from warmer regions tend to be heavier, even thick wines. Many have a tinge of sweet.

Zinfandel Rosé. *(Zin fan DELL Roe ZAY)* A varietal pink table wine, usually dry and delicate of flavor. It is dry and crisp enough to go with red meats when a hot day suggests a light, chilled wine rather than a heartier, warmer red.

California Varietal RED Wines

California Varietal RED Wines	Southern California — BROOKSIDE	CALLAWAY	J. FILIPPI	FIRESTONE	HOFFMAN	OPICI	PESENTI	SAN ANTONIO	THOMAS	YORK MOUNTAIN	South of San Francisco Bay — ALMADEN	BARGETTO	BERTERO	BONESIO	DAVID BRUCE	CHALONE	CONCANNON	ENZ	FORTINO	GEMELLO—FILICE	GUGLIELMO-MT. MADONNA	HECKER PASS	THOMAS KRUSE	LLORDS & ELWOOD	J. LOHR	PAUL MASSON	MIRASSOU	MONTEREY PENINSULA	THE MONTEREY VINEYARD	MT. EDEN	NEPENTHE	NICASIO	NOVITIATE	PEDRIZZETTI	RIDGE	ROUDON-SMITH	SAN MARTIN	SHERRILL CELLARS	VILLA ARMANDO	WEIBEL	WENTE BROS.	WOODSIDE
ALICANTE-BOUSCHET																																										
BARBERA			●					●	●		●		●	●						●			●			●		●			●			●		●			●			
CABERNET SAUVIGNON	●	●	●		●	●		●	●	●	●		●	●	●		●		●	●		●	●		●	●	●	●	●	●	●	●	●	●	●	●	●	●	●	●		
CARIGNANE																			●			●	●								●											
CHARBONO																																										
GAMAY																																		●					●			
GAMAY BEAUJOLAIS	●		●			●		●			●									●	●					●	●		●		●										●	●
GRENACHE											●				●				●																							
GRIGNOLINO													●	●						●														●								
MERLOT													●																													
PETITE SIRAH	●	●						●			●				●		●		●	●	●	●	●	●	●						●			●	●	●	●			●		
PINOT NOIR			●		●	●		●	●	●	●		●	●	●		●			●			●	●		●	●	●		●				●	●		●			●	●	●
PINOT ST. GEORGE	●																●							●																		
RUBY CABERNET					●	●					●	●							●	●	●					●								●			●		●			
ZINFANDEL	●	●	●		●	●	●	●	●	●	●	●	●	●	●		●		●	●	●	●				●	●				●	●	●	●	●	●	●	●	●	●	●	●

Varietal ROSÉ Wines

Varietal ROSÉ Wines	BROOKSIDE	CALLAWAY	J. FILIPPI	FIRESTONE	HOFFMAN	OPICI	PESENTI	SAN ANTONIO	THOMAS	YORK MOUNTAIN	ALMADEN	BARGETTO	BERTERO	BONESIO	DAVID BRUCE	CHALONE	CONCANNON	ENZ	FORTINO	GEMELLO—FILICE	GUGLIELMO-MT. MADONNA	HECKER PASS	THOMAS KRUSE	LLORDS & ELWOOD	J. LOHR	PAUL MASSON	MIRASSOU	MONTEREY PENINSULA	THE MONTEREY VINEYARD	MT. EDEN	NEPENTHE	NICASIO	NOVITIATE	PEDRIZZETTI	RIDGE	ROUDON-SMITH	SAN MARTIN	SHERRILL CELLARS	VILLA ARMANDO	WEIBEL	WENTE BROS.	WOODSIDE
CABERNET SAUVIGNON				●				●															●	●																		
GAMAY																									●																	
GRENACHE		●			●			●			●		●							●		●	●								●		●						●		●	
GRIGNOLINO																							●																			
PETITE SIRAH																										●					●											
ZINFANDEL													●		●		●	●					●													●					●	

Sonoma and Mendocino: CAMBIASO · CHATEAU ST. JEAN · CRESTA BLANCA · DRY CREEK · EDMEADES · FETZER · FOPPIANO · GEYSER PEAK · GRAND CRU · HACIENDA · HANZELL · HUSCH · ITALIAN SWISS COLONY · JOHNSON'S · KENWOOD · KORBEL · MARTINI & PRATI · PARDUCCI · PASTORI · J. PEDRONCELLI · RUSSIAN RIVER · SEBASTIANI · SIMI · SONOMA VINEYARDS · SOUVERAIN · J. SWAN · TRENTADUE · Z-D

Napa and Solano: BEAULIEU · BERINGER/LOS HERMANOS · BURGESS · CADENASSO · CARNEROS CREEK · CAYMUS · CHAPPELLET · CHARLES KRUG · CHATEAU MONTELENA · THE CHRISTIAN BROTHERS · CLOS DU VAL · CUVAISON · DIAMOND CREEK · FRANCISCAN · FREEMARK ABBEY · HEITZ · INGLENOOK

(Continued on next page)

Napa and Solano (Continued) — Central Valley and Gold Country

California Varietal RED Wines (Cont'd.)	LOUIS M. MARTINI	MAYACAMAS	ROBERT MONDAVI	MOUNT VEEDER	NICHELINI	OAKVILLE	JOSEPH PHELPS	POPE VALLEY	SPRING MOUNTAIN	STAG'S LEAP	STERLING	STONEGATE	SUTTER HOME	CONRAD VIANO	VILLA MT. EDEN	WOODEN VALLEY	YVERDON	AMADOR	BARENGO	BEAR MT.-M. LAMONT	BRONCO	BUTTE CREEK	CADLOLO	CALIFORNIA GROWERS	CALIFORNIA WINE ASSN.	COLUMBIA	D'AGOSTINI	DELICATO	EAST-SIDE/CONTI ROYALE	FICKLIN	FRANZIA	E. & J. GALLO	GIUMARRA	GOLD HILL	LANDIS	MONTEVINA	A. NONINI	…
ALICANTE-BOUSCHET																																						
BARBERA	●													●		●			●					●	●			●				●	●			●	●	
CABERNET SAUVIGNON	●	●	●	●	●	●	●	●	●	●	●	●		●	●	●			●		●		●	●	●			●										
CARIGNANE						●																																●
CHARBONO																																						●
GAMAY			●		●	●								●	●																							
GAMAY BEAUJOLAIS	●										●					●	●		●						●			●										
GRENACHE																		●																				
GRIGNOLINO																																						
MERLOT	●										●	●																										
PETITE SIRAH			●			●	●	●				●							●											●			●					
PINOT NOIR	●		●			●	●	●			●	●		●					●			●		●				●										
PINOT ST. GEORGE																																						
RUBY CABERNET							●																	●	●	●					●	●	●	●	●			
ZINFANDEL	●	●	●	●	●	●	●	●	●		●				●	●	●	●	●	●	●		●	●	●	●	●	●	●		●	●	●	●	●	●	●	●

Varietal ROSÉ Wines

	LOUIS M. MARTINI	MAYACAMAS	ROBERT MONDAVI	MOUNT VEEDER	NICHELINI	OAKVILLE	JOSEPH PHELPS	POPE VALLEY	SPRING MOUNTAIN	STAG'S LEAP	STERLING	STONEGATE	SUTTER HOME	CONRAD VIANO	VILLA MT. EDEN	WOODEN VALLEY	YVERDON	AMADOR	BARENGO	BEAR MT.-M. LAMONT	BRONCO	BUTTE CREEK	CADLOLO	CALIFORNIA GROWERS	CALIFORNIA WINE ASSN.	COLUMBIA	D'AGOSTINI	DELICATO	EAST-SIDE/CONTI ROYALE	FICKLIN	FRANZIA	E. & J. GALLO	GIUMARRA	GOLD HILL	LANDIS	MONTEVINA	A. NONINI	…
CABERNET SAUVIGNON										●																												
GAMAY	●		●			●																●																
GRENACHE																				●			●	●	●			●	●		●		●					
GRIGNOLINO																																						
PETITE SIRAH																																						
ZINFANDEL		●						●						●																								

California Varietal WHITE Wines	Southern California									South of San Francisco Bay																											
	BROOKSIDE	CALLAWAY	J. FILIPPI	FIRESTONE	HOFFMAN	OPICI	SAN ANTONIO	THOMAS	YORK MOUNTAIN	ALMADEN	BARGETTO	BERTERO	BONESIO	DAVID BRUCE	CHALONE	CONCANNON	ENZ	FORTINO	GEMELLO—FILICE	GUGLIELMO-MT. MADONNA	THOMAS KRUSE	LIVE OAKS	LLORDS & ELWOOD	J. LOHR	PAUL MASSON	MIRASSOU	MONTEREY PENINSULA	THE MONTEREY VINEYARD	MT. EDEN	NEPENTHE	NICASIO	NOVITIATE	PEDRIZZETTI	RIDGE	ROUDON-SMITH	SAN MARTIN	SHERRILL CELLARS
CHARDONNAY (or Pinot Chardonnay)	●		●		●	●	●		●	●	●			●	●						●		●	●	●	●	●	●	●	●	●		●	●	●	●	
CHENIN BLANC (or Pineau or White Pinot)	●	●	●		●	●	●	●	●	●	●	●	●		●	●			●			●	●	●	●	●		●				●	●		●	●	●
EMERALD RIESLING	●						●																									●				●	
FLORA											●																										
FOLLE BLANCHE																																					
FRENCH COLOMBARD	●						●		●	●	●				●				●							●											
GEWURZTRAMINER			●							●		●														●										●	
GREEN HUNGARIAN			●			●	●	●																										●			
GREY RIESLING										●	●		●																								
GOLDEN CHASSELAS																	●				●																
JOHANNISBERG RIESLING (or White Riesling)	●	●	●	●	●	●	●		●	●	●			●		●			●				●		●	●			●	●	●	●	●	●	●	●	●
MUSCAT (light)											●					●					●											●				●	
PINOT BLANC										●	●					●									●	●			●								
SAUVIGNON BLANC (or Blanc Fumé, Fumé Blanc)		●								●		●				●								●											●		
SAUVIGNON VERT																					●																
SEMILLON										●						●																●				●	
SYLVANER										●		●						●										●						●		●	
* RIESLING			●		●		●																		●	●											
ST. EMILION	●																																				
TRAMINER																																					
WHITE ZINFANDEL														●																				●			

* The terms Sylvaner and Riesling can be interchangeable, but are not wholly synonymous.

(Continued on next page)

California Varietal WHITE Wines (Cont'd.)	South of San Francisco Bay (Continued)				Sonoma and Mendocino																															
	VILLA ARMANDO	WEIBEL	WENTE BROS.	WOODSIDE	BUENA VISTA	DAVIS BYNUM	CAMBIASO	CHATEAU ST. JEAN	CRESTA BLANCA	DRY CREEK	EDMEADES	FETZER	FOPPIANO	GEYSER PEAK	GRAND CRU	HACIENDA	HANZELL	HUSCH	ITALIAN SWISS COLONY	JOHNSON'S	KENWOOD	KORBEL	MARTINI & PRATI	PARDUCCI	PASTORI	J. PEDRONCELLI	RUSSIAN RIVER	SEBASTIANI	SIMI	SONOMA VINEYARDS	SOUVERAIN	TRENTADUE	Z-D	BEAULIEU	BERINGER/LOS HERMANOS	BURGESS
CHARDONNAY (or Pinot Chardonnay)		●	●	●	●	●		●	●	●		●		●		●	●	●			●	●		●		●	●	●	●	●	●	●	●	●	●	●
CHENIN BLANC (or Pineau or White Pinot)	●	●		●	●	●			●	●				●		●	●	●			●	●		●	●	●				●	●	●			●	●
EMERALD RIESLING																																				
FLORA																								●												
FOLLE BLANCHE																																				
FRENCH COLOMBARD						●	●	●			●		●			●				●				●							●	●	●			
GEWURZTRAMINER					●			●	●	●				●	●			●						●		●		●	●				●			
GREEN HUNGARIAN		●			●			●			●										●							●								●
GREY RIESLING		●	●		●																		●	●	●					●	●	●			●	
GOLDEN CHASSELAS																																	●			
JOHANNISBERG RIESLING (or White Riesling)	●	●			●	●	●							●		●					●	●		●	●					●	●	●		●	●	●
MUSCAT (light)							●																						●							
PINOT BLANC	●		●		●																			●												
SAUVIGNON BLANC (or Blanc Fumé, Fumé Blanc)			●			●		●	●	●		●	●											●								●		●	●	
SAUVIGNON VERT																																●				
SEMILLON			●																													●				
SYLVANER					●																		●	●			●									
* RIESLING																								●												
ST. EMILION																																				
TRAMINER																																				
WHITE ZINFANDEL										●																										

* The terms Sylvaner and Riesling can be interchangeable, but are not wholly synonymous.

Napa and Solano																											Central Valley and Gold Country															
CHAPPELET	CHARLES KRUG	CHATEAU MONTELENA	THE CHRISTIAN BROTHERS	CUVAISON	FRANCISCAN	FREEMARK ABBEY	HEITZ	INGLENOOK	LOUIS M. MARTINI	MAYACAMAS	ROBERT MONDAVI	MOUNT VEEDER	NICHELINI	OAKVILLE	JOSEPH PHELPS	POPE VALLEY	SPRING MOUNTAIN	STAG'S LEAP	STERLING	STONEGATE	STONY HILL	SUTTER HOME	CONRAD VIANO	VILLA MT. EDEN	WOODEN VALLEY	YVERDON	BARENGO	BEAR MT.-M. LAMONT	BRONCO	BUTTE CREEK	CADLOLO	CALIFORNIA GROWERS	CALIFORNIA WINE ASSN.	D'AGOSTINI	DELICATO	EAST-SIDE/CONTI ROYALE	FICKLIN	E. & J. GALLO	GIUMARRA	GOLD HILL	MONTEVINA	A. PAPAGNI	WINEMASTERS GUILD

Putting wine to the test

EVALUATION SHEET

WINE	'69 Zinfandel		'68 Zinfandel	
APPEARANCE 0-2	brilliant	2	very clear	2
COLOR 0-2	too light	1½	medium red	2
AROMA & BOUQUET 0-4	vinous only	2	vinous, faintly varietal	3
ACESCENCE 0-2	none	2	none	2
TOTAL ACID 0-2	a bit high	1	pleasing	2
SUGAR 0-1	dry	1	good balance with acid	1
BODY 0-1	good	1	slightly thin	1
FLAVOR 0-2	medium	1	light, clean	1
ASTRINGENCY 0-2	rough	2	good	2
GENERAL QUALITY 0-2	average	1	average	1
TOTAL		14½		17

```
17-20 Wine of outstanding characteristics
13-16 Sound commercial wine -- no outstanding merit or defect
10-12 Commercially acceptable wine with noticeable defect
0-9  Commercially unacceptable wine
```

Wine is more than the sum of its parts, but a scoring system that tries to add up a sum is one of the most useful ways for people to improve their tasting skills and thereby their appreciation of good wine.

The 20-point scorecard shown here was developed by faculty members at the University of California at Davis for professional use. It has an impressive record of working for amateurs as well as for professionals.

At first there is a temptation to score wines very low. It is the same sort of feeling that prompts music critics on country weeklies to knock the New York Philharmonic. The fear is to look less sage than the types downtown. Tasting with a genuinely knowledgeable veteran is the fastest cure for such fears as well as the best way to learn the individual characteristics of wines.

With or without experienced coaching, the card has become a useful buying guide as soon as sound, enjoyable wines begin scoring 14 to 16 points. The card works best in comparative blind tastings—where several bottles are masked to hide their identities—but the scorecard can be used one bottle at a time to help make orderly evaluation of a wine's good and not-so-good qualities.

This is how it goes:

Appearance (2). Give the full 2 points if the wine is *brilliant* with no sign of particles or murkiness (be sure any particles aren't bits of cork). If the wine isn't quite sparkling and has a few floating particles, consider it *clear* and give 1 point. If the wine is *dull* or *cloudy*, give it 0.

Color (2). You need some concept of what color is right for a wine.

Acceptable colors for white wines include *yellow*, *gold*, and *straw color*. Some new whites show an acceptable *greenish* cast. Flaws are *amber* tones (accompanied by a Sherrylike odor), or a *bleached* look at the edges from overuse of sulfur dioxide (accompanied by a distinctive odor). Take away 1 point if either of these flaws is noticeable; 2 points if it is pronounced. Or score the full 2 points if the color is acceptable.

A rosé can be a distinct pink and—depending on the grape from which it is made—have a suggestion of red or orange. But violet tints, brown (amber) tones, and a *low red* color (almost as deep as a red wine) are faults.

The color of red wines depends greatly on the variety of grape and maturity of the wine. Pinot Noir may be light enough to describe as *low red*, or light red. New reds and blends often have blue to purple tints, but these *high red*, or deep red, shadings may also come from other factors adversely affecting wine quality.

Medium red is the standard of red wine color and is expected in a Zinfandel or Cabernet Sauvignon. Amber to brown tones might indicate age or perhaps oxidation (with the Sherrylike or baked odor also found in oxidized white wines).

Reduce points only if unacceptable tints or tones begin to predominate.

Aroma and Bouquet (4). Aroma has to do with odors that come from the grape. Bouquet refers to odors that develop after the wine is made. You'll need help in separating these two and in pinpointing what's distinctive.

Aroma may be *vinous* (smells like wine made from grapes, but without varietal character), *distinct* (when some varietal attributes come through), or *varietal* (when the particular grape variety is unmistakable). The intensity of aroma may be *light*, *medium*, or *high*. Give a wine 2 points for being pleasantly vinous, 3 for having

THE WHOLE FLAVOR. Acute "tasting" of a wine starts with the eyes and depends far more heavily on the nose than it does on the palate. The scorecard explains why.

some varietal overtones, 4 if it has unmistakable varietal aroma. This score holds if factors in the bouquet don't start taking away any points.

Bouquet is almost impossible to describe positively; only experience makes it obvious. But it is what you smell in the wine that is not the smell of the grape. Negative factors are off odors that might be described as alcoholic, excessively woody, moldy, mousy, corked, or sulfur dioxide. All these indicate that something went awry in the making of the wine.

Acescence (2). This is the term for volatile acid. Do you smell vinegar? If not, give the wine 2 points. If there is a faint vinegar aroma, give it 1. If it is strong, give it 0.

(When judging several wines together, it is wise to rate each one this far down the score card before tasting any.)

Total acid (2). You've now earned your first sip of the wine—but you mustn't swallow yet. You can't smell total acid, you have to feel it. If the sugar level of the wine (next step) is in harmony with the acid and the amounts are appropriate for the type of wine, your mouth should feel rather refreshed. If the total acid is low, there is a sensation of flatness, flabbiness, or even soapiness. If the total acid is high, there's a sensation of unpleasant sharpness. The intensity of either fault determines how much you take off.

Sugar (1). Again, sugar and total acid must go hand in hand. But if the wine seems overly sweet for the type, this is a fault. And if the wine is overly dry (non-sweet) for the type, total acid will dominate noticeably.

Body (1). This describes the feel of the wine as it is swished about in the mouth. Does it fill your mouth with tastes? Or does it seem thin and watery, or too heavy? Now swallow your wine; does it leave a lingering after-taste, or is it quickly forgotten? If the wine has the light, medium, or full body appropriate for its type (experience or an expert must guide you), give it the point.

Flavor (2). Does the flavor correspond with the smell of the wine—*fruity, clean, full, balanced*? This is worth 2 points if the wine also smells good; less if there are off tastes such as *metallic, stemmy, hot*. The taste that lingers in your mouth after you swallow the wine is an important consideration.

Astringency (2). Tannins can make your mouth feel rough or puckery. Limited amounts are acceptable in some whites, not in others. Young reds have more pronounced tannins than mature reds. In astringency, whites might be *smooth, slightly rough*. Reds might also be *medium rough, rough,* or *very rough*. Either reds or whites might be *soft, mellow, velvety, rounded, hard,* or *harsh*. A young red shouldn't be faulted too much for being rough, provided that it is a "big" wine that should age well and appropriately for its type.

General quality (2). Does one sip call for another? Does the wine have what might be called "comehitherness"? How it rates in terms of this kind of appeal is one measure of its general quality.

But some wine judges also use general quality as one of their "fudge factors" (along with aroma and bouquet, and flavor), especially when dealing in half-points to make a total score come out right. In other words, you might add up all the other points, then use these 2 points to put the wine in the category in which you feel it really belongs.

For straight, no-fudge scoring: If the wine is above average in general quality, give it 2 points; if average, 1 point; below average, 0 points.

Keeping wine at home

Most of the dedicated wine hobbyists in the world began by keeping a few bottles in a rack in one corner of the dining room, or maybe in a case box in the basement.

Wine is a living thing, just as the romantic literature says it is. Wherever bottles are kept, their owner will profit by paying reasonable attention to four conditions: temperature, light, motion, and the relative position of the stored bottles. The more expensive the wine and the longer it is kept, the more important these conditions become.

TEMPERATURE: The quoted ideal is about 58°F for table wines, perhaps a few degrees warmer for dessert wines and a few degrees cooler for sparkling wines. For shorter terms than five years, temperatures within the range of 50-75° should not harm well made wine so long as the fluctuations are gradual and not daily.

LIGHT: Sun rays, fluorescent lamps and other sources of ultraviolet light are harmful to the flavors of all wine. Wines meant for long aging should be kept entirely away from both. Those to be consumed within one or two years can endure anything but direct sun.

MOTION: There should be very little, and no rapid vibrations such as caused by storing the wine around washers, dryers, freezers, and the like.

BOTTLE POSITION: Air is an implacable enemy of wine. It causes a Sherried taste (oxidation), and permits the growth of vinegar bacteria. For this reason, bottles with bark corks should be stored on their sides, or with their necks tilted slightly downward. (Full upside down may result in sediment sticking to the cork after a time.) On the other hand, bottles with plastic or plastic-lined metal caps should be stored upright, so no wine touches the cap. After a time the liner or cap may impart off-flavors to wine in contact with it.

THE RIGHT WAY. Wine Cellar at Sunset's Menlo Park headquarters exemplifies proper storage conditions as described on this page.

Index

This book was printed and bound by Graphic Arts Center, Portland, Oregon, from
litho film prepared by Balzer-Shopes Litho Plate Company, San Francisco. Body type
is Patina and News Gothic; heads are Melior, composed by Atherton's Advertising
Typography, Inc., Palo Alto, California. Paper for pages is Velvo Enamel made by
Westvaco, Luke, Maryland.